SEXUAL AWARENESS

SEXUAL AWARENESS
A PRACTICAL APPROACH

Barry W. McCarthy

Mary Ryan

Fred A. Johnson

Boyd & Fraser Publishing Company

The Scrimshaw Press, Inc.

San Francisco

1975

Library of Congress Cataloging in Publication Data
McCarthy, Barry W   1943-
Sexual Awareness.

1. Sex.   2. College students — Sexual behavior.
I. Ryan, Mary, 1937-   joint author. II. Johnson,
Fred A., 1941-   joint author. III. Title.
HQ35.2.M3   301.41'8   75p8841
ISBN 0-912020-43-1
ISBN 0-87835-048-9 pbk.

Composition by The Cal-Central Press
Printing and Binding by The Banta West Company
Design by James Stockton Graphic Design
Illustration by Pat Maloney

Contents

Introduction

1 Enhancing Sexual Awareness and Comfort   p. 1

2 A Self-Exploration and Enhancement Program for Women   p. 15

3 A Self-Exploration and Enhancement Program for Men   p. 33

4 Pleasuring Using Non-Genital Touching   p. 45

5 Genital Touching and Pleasuring   p. 61

6 Increasing Arousal and Sexual Response for Women   p. 77

7 Increasing Vaginal Feeling and Response   p. 97

8 Increasing Arousal and Potency for Men   p. 105

9 Learning Ejaculatory Control   p. 121

10 Increasing Enjoyment of Oral-Genital Stimulation   p. 137

11 Increasing Comfort with Non-Demand Pleasuring   p. 153

12 Sexual Expression for the Aging Couple   p. 165

13 Increasing Comfort with Sexual Intercourse   p. 179

14 The Concept of Sexual Therapy   p. 207

Suggested Readings for Further Information

Introduction

Many books about sex have been made available to laymen and professionals over the past few years. Most of these publications are of the "cookbook" variety, containing lists of sophisticated techniques to use to improve one's sexual life. In our work in sexual dysfunction therapy, we often saw couples who had read such books; usually, they found that these cookbooks caused more harm than good. When we studied some recent technique-oriented sex books, we discovered that they were not written for a typical or average individual or couple, but rather were compilations of sophisticated techniques more suitable for highly-experienced people. Ordinary people could read about these sexual techniques, but they were usually unable to integrate them into their own sexual lives. Thus they were left feeling even less comfortable than before with their own sexuality.

We tried to take a different approach in this book. Our key emphasis centers on the typical person or couple. Our book is oriented toward the person and couple who wish to understand and enhance their sexual feelings and functioning. One does not need any sexual dysfunction or hangup to benefit from this book. In effect, it is a basic book designed to build and emphasize a healthy view of sexuality. It is based on these premises:

1. You are a sexual person from the day you are born until the day you die.
2. Sexuality is an integral part of your personality.
3. Comfort with your own body and with sexual expression is the basis of sexual responsibility.
4. Your sexuality should enhance your life.

Our book does contain information about the most common of the sexual problems. This is not a do-it-yourself therapy book, however. It can give you a new and positive view toward solving sexual problems — a view that could be very helpful to you. As other professionals do, we use the exercises that we present as an adjunct to sexual-dysfunction therapy. Therefore, this book can also be valuable to sex therapists and counselors, marriage counselors, psychologists, psychiatrists, and social workers. However, it is not necessary to have or to be dealing with a sexual problem in order to read and benefit from our book. The exercises can result in both enhancement and prevention of some forms of dysfunction. In this last respect, we see the following chapters as particularly relevant: "Sexual Expression for the Aging Couple"; "Increasing Enjoyment of Oral-Genital Stimulation"; and "Increasing Comfort with Non-Demand Pleasuring."

We want to thank our students who took the Human Sexual Behavior class at American University and Montgomery College for their interest in, and constructive suggestions about, this book. Also, we are grateful to our clients and friends who shared with us their learnings and feelings of sensual and sexual enhancement as a result of using our exercises. Special thanks go to Diana Humphreys, who did an exceptional job with the original editing of this text. We wish to include thanks to Blake Chaffee for his contribution to the writing. We also owe a debt of gratitude to Emily Waterman Stimson and Marianna Taylor, who typed revision after revision of these pages.

More than anyone else, however, we wish to thank the wives, husbands, lovers, and children who granted us the permission to work hard and long on this book. Writing it has been a worthwhile experience for us, because we have learned more about and have felt more comfortable with our own sensual and sexual responses.

We hope that reading and using our book can help you as a person and you as a couple to enhance your own feelings about yourselves as sensual and sexual people.

1 Enhancing Sexual Awareness and Comfort

Both directly and indirectly, the media convey the impression that a great sexual revolution is taking place, that everybody is enjoying sex, and that the key to being truly sexually liberated is to be able to engage in a wide variety of esoteric sexual activities. On the contrary, the majority of American individuals and couples find that this is far from the true picture. Instead, the scientific evidence indicates that approximately 50% of married couples are having major difficulties in their sexual functioning, and that young couples have many of the same types of difficulties with sexual functioning as do older couples. People talk more frequently and openly about sex than ever before; however, their feelings and behavior have not kept up with liberalized attitudes.

This book is designed to help individuals and couples enhance their sexual communication, feelings, and functioning. It is oriented toward increasing basic sexual awareness and comfort for the average individual and couple. The book emphasizes basic skills and techniques; it does not focus on esoteric procedures and unusual approaches.

Sexual intercourse is only one part of our broader sexuality, and our sexuality is an integral part of our personality. In our culture, we have never really appreciated and promoted our sexuality in positive ways. Rather, for most people, sexuality has been a source of conflict, guilt, and related problems. In this book we emphasize the view that sex and sexuality should be used to enhance our feelings about ourselves as persons and to help us relate more comfortably and positively to other people than we have before.

UNDERSTANDING AND ACCEPTANCE OF SEXUALITY

The beginning of good sexual adjustment is understanding and acceptance of yourself, your body, your sensual feelings, and your sexual feelings. For most people, in growing up and learning about themselves and their social environment there were two very important negative teachings about sex. The first was that sex is basically bad, and that it becomes good only if it is used in the context of marriage. The second was that sex refers almost exclusively to intercourse. Our viewpoint is that sex is basically good and an integral part of every person. Sex is much more than just intercourse. It is everything from an affectionate glance to a gentle caress on the arm to a loving and comfortable afterplay.

We set out to write this book, first because there was a real need in the areas of sexual enhancement and solution of sexual problems. That need was for a book that clearly outlined the basic components of sexual awareness, comfort, and technique. Furthermore, the typical nonprofessional audience is actively seeking such a guide.

We oriented our book toward learning about and enhancing positive attitudes toward sexuality, *but not toward do-it-yourself sexual therapy*. The exercises are meant to give the individual and couple a chance to try some alternative sexual experiences and techniques, but there is no requirement that they must all be tried or that the reader must become proficient in any particular techniques.

Second, for individuals who are experiencing a sexual problem or dysfunction, we wrote this book not to provide a do-it-yourself therapy, but to expand their understanding and experience in sexuality. Marriage counselors and sex therapists can use the book as an adjunct to treatment for their clients. We have used the exercises in that context with our own clients.

The third reason for writing this book was to reach educational audiences, both college students and advanced students in the helping areas such as psychology, medicine, marriage counseling, social work, and the ministry. If students can learn to develop an awareness and a comfort with sensuality and sexuality, their own lives and the lives of clients with whom they work can be much improved. Our belief is that education is the best means by which to remedy or prevent the harm that may come from sex myths and negative attitudes toward sexuality. Our hope is that this book is a step toward educational progress in these areas.

SOURCES FOR OUR MODEL

In this book we utilize an approach that comes from two different sources: the research of Masters and Johnson and the work of psychologists in social learning techniques. Masters and Johnson are the most eminent workers in the sex research and sex therapy fields. Their pioneering work has increased our knowledge of sexual behavior tremendously, both in the study of the physiology of human sexual response and in introducing a treatment approach to sexual dysfunction. They have also dispelled some of the myths that have caused great psychological damage to millions of men and women.

The social learning approach comes from the field of psychology. It consists of a series of techniques to help people learn new skills and attitudes. The major premise is that the best way to learn is through a gradual step-by-step method, making sure one is comfortable with the first exercise before he moves on to the next, and utilizing supportive and constructive feedback to help the learning process. Also, the process must be enjoyable and reinforcing or rewarding.

MUTUAL COMFORT AND SUPPORT

As you will notice, we do not even talk about sexual intercourse *per se* until almost the end of the book. This is because we have found that most couples put too much emphasis on intercourse and orgasm, and that this overemphasis interferes with the full expression of their sexuality. From our perspective, if a couple is comfortable with themselves and with each other, with their feelings of sensuality and their ability to give and receive sexual pleasure, then intercourse and orgasm will be a natural culmination of their sexual activity. Notice that throughout the book there is constant emphasis on *slow, gentle, tender, rhythmic,* and *flowing* touching and pleasuring. To us these are essential ingredients for sexual satisfaction. When these are present in foreplay, intercourse, and afterplay, the couple reports much more satisfaction and enjoyment than as a result of any esoteric sexual technique or acrobatic position.

Remember, our book is *not* a self-help sex therapy device. It cannot replace the skills and understanding of a professional counselor. Instead, our book is both an aid and a guide for those who can communicate well and who can benefit from our suggestions.

Couples who are experiencing interpersonal conflict, communication problems, severe sex difficulties involving one or both partners, or those who have current or previous psychological difficulties, might profit far more from seeking professional help than from working together on the exercises in this book. Also, others who might seek professional help more profitably instead of using this book alone are those couples in which one partner is enthusiastic and the other is hesitant; where one or both feel that having a professional third person could help the learning process; or, where one or both would rather develop individual programs instead of the ones presented here. These exercises are intended to *enhance basic responses* to sensual and sexual feelings. If there is any question of physical or medical impairments or problems, we suggest consulting a physician. Although sexual difficulties rarely have a physical basis, it is worth examining that possibility.

THE CONCEPT OF EXERCISES

These materials were originally developed in the context of sexual therapy. In fact, they were first written because we saw a couple only once a week; our clients needed structured exercises during the week to help them focus on changing their sexual attitudes and behaviors. We decided to utilize exercises independently of sexual therapy when we realized that well-functioning individuals and couples — people who would never consider themselves as candidates for sexual therapy — could get a good deal of benefit from such exercises.

Also, couples who simply need to learn to be more comfortable in communicating with each other about what they want, what feels good, and what they prefer sexually could probably use our exercises more profitably than sexual therapy. Rather than focusing on problems alone, our approach provides a way of preventing communication difficulties and sexual problems by helping each person and couple enhance their communication and sexuality.

Additional information on the general subject of sex therapy is provided in the last chapter of this book.

We suggest that you decide whether our approach to enhancing sexual awareness and comfort might be appropriate for you. If you decide that marital or sexual therapy would be more appropriate, we suggest that you seek professional therapy. You may want to use our exercises only in conjunction with the therapist's suggestions. If you are unsure of the appropriateness of the program for you, you might read through the chapter on non-genital touching and then discuss it with your partner. We recommend that you not proceed with doing exercises unless both you and your partner have discussed both the exercises and your expectations about them and have agreed that they would be good for you as a couple.

THE AUDIENCE FOR THIS BOOK

People without regular partners are encouraged to read the book to learn about new sexual behaviors and to change their attitudes toward sexuality, but it is our feeling that a good relationship between partners is essential to achieve benefit from the exercises themselves. Thus, it is better simply to read the material than to attempt to use the exercises with someone with whom a good relationship does not exist.

Our exercises were written mainly (but not exclusively) with the married couple in mind — expecially the couple who relate well to one another but who find that they have a good deal of misunderstanding in the area of sex, including also noncommunication and poor sexual techniques. However, these exercises have been used successfully by others as well. They have been found enhancing for couples not married (but who have a commitment to their relationship and to improving their sexual communication). We have been particularly gratified to find the exercises used successfully among couples fifty and older — couples who found that the exercises helped them to reawaken and to resensitize sensual and sexual feelings.

We feel that our chapter on sexual functioning in aging is of particular import, because this is a neglected area. People can function sexually into their seventies, eighties, and later. The idea that sex belongs to the young is one of the most cruel sex myths.

In addition, our exercises have been used by homosexual couples. Although the exercises are aimed toward heterosexual couples, we find that they are just as applicable to gay people, with very few modifications. Of course, we believe that our exercises can be used by sexually well-functioning couples, since we can all benefit from enhancing our experiences with sensual and sexual response and sharing the enhancement with our partner.

PROCEDURE FOR EXERCISES

For couples who feel that the exercises in our book would be valuable for them, we suggest the following procedure:

Begin by deciding what you want to learn about yourself and your partner.

Be aware that the best way to learn sexually is to understand your own reactions first, then to give feedback and to guide your partner. Among the best ways to give feedback to your partner are the following:

1. Be supportive and constructive.
2. Give positive feedback before negative.
3. Be specific.
4. When giving negative feedback, request the change that you would like rather than making a negative comment about your partner as a person.
5. Support your partner in making the changes you request.

Agree on how much time you will be able to spend on the exercises during the week.

Exercises As Guidelines

The exercises should be regarded as guidelines rather than as rigid, unyielding rules. If you start seeing the exercises as required homework or as something you must do, you will probably get little enjoyment or benefit from them. Use the exercises as guidelines to help you explore, learn, accept, and ultimately to feel comfortable with your sensual and sexual feelings and behavior. The exercises are meant to give you choices and alternatives to experience and to find what you as a person and as couple find good for you. To enhance sensual and sexual functioning, it is important to be spontaneous, to try out different things, to share and to communicate comfortably, and to vary your approaches. For instance, we emphasize the importance of slow, tender, gentle, rhythmic, and flowing touching. However, if that is the only style of touching you use, it may become quite boring. At times, each partner may like rapid, intense, or focused touching. In the same way, we suggest sometimes showering or bathing together. However, it can be good to enjoy sex while you are both sweaty. Sensations seem to be enhanced by natural body essences. Variety and spontaniety are two major ingredients in enhancing sensual and sexual interaction.

Exercise Organization: How To Use These Exercises

Most sections of the book are divided into four sets of exercises.* This four-fold division is intended to increase skill and comfort levels gradually. You can feel free to move at your own pace; however, be aware that sensual and sexual feelings develop slowly. Pushing too fast is a very common problem. A good suggestion for the couple is to move together, rather than for one partner to try to push the other.

*Chapter 2 contains a double set of exercises.

Basis Of The Exercises

The core of the sexual awareness and comfort exercises consists of
(1) non-genital touching and (2) genital touching and pleasuring.
From these experiences you can really develop your awareness of
sensual and sexual feelings; exchange feedback with your partner;
learn to be comfortable both giving and receiving pleasure; learn to
initiate and respond to sexual interactions; and develop your ability
to give and appreciate slow, gentle, tender, rhythmic, flowing
touching. These principles are the foundation of a healthy sexuality.
Without a feeling of comfort with this foundation, you will find that
the other exercises will lack value.

Avoiding Goal Orientation

We would suggest that you devote at least two weeks to the initial
exercises, and that during that time you consider refraining from
intercourse. So much sexual activity is goal-oriented and
intercourse-oriented that sensual and sexual awareness are most
difficult to develop. Our feeling is that two weeks away from
intercourse is well worth the effort to help you attain improved
feelings about the whole of sensual and sexual expression. In fact, we
recommend that once a month or once every other month, couples
spend time in a variety of non-genital and genital pleasuring not
culminating in intercourse. In this way, they continue to be aware
that not all touching must be goal-directed. Intercourse is not the
only means of sexual expression; through the exercises you will
probably realize this fact for yourself and with your partner.

During the same week you are involved together as
a couple with non-genital and genital pleasuring exercises, we
recommend that you engage in the self-exploration and
enhancement exercises individually. Both men and women are not
as aware of, and comfortable with, their own bodily, sensual and
sexual responses as they could be. Accepting and being comfortable

with oneself is the basis for sharing with one's partner. We recommend that you do the self-exploration exercises at your own pace. You should concentrate on the areas and techniques you feel you need to learn more about.

A good guideline for self-awareness exercises (and all other exercises in this book) is never to do anything that causes you a great deal of discomfort. Move slowly and do not proceed to the next step until you are comfortable with the preceding step. Remember, the exercises are meant to be enjoyable learning experiences. The second reason for self-exploration and enhancement is that, if you want it, self-enhancement may provide an orgasmic outlet during the two-week period mentioned above.

Flexibility

Be as flexible as you wish in using the exercises. We suggest that you read through a whole chapter first by yourself. Then discuss it with your partner. Together read through a single exercise and then decide if and when you want to proceed with it. During the exercises, some people keep the book nearby, while others improvise as they go along. Some couples will go through each exercise step-by-step, while others will combine two or more exercises. Decide what procedure is most comfortable for you as a couple. The most important ingredient in keeping the exercises as a positive learning and sharing experience is feedback between you and your partner. Remember to think of the exercises as flexible guidelines and to use them to enhance your sexual functioning, attitudes, and feelings.

COMMUNICATION

Sexual therapists agree that communication is a key to good sexual growth, adjustment, and happiness. In our culture, and in others as well, it is hard to articulate one's feelings. After the first romantic conversations and messages, it seems, a curtain falls between lovers; for some few the reduction in communication is slight, and they find other ways to express their feelings. For most people, however, the curtain is heavy and dark. Thoreau spoke for modern man when he wrote over a hundred years ago, "The mass of men lead lives of quiet desperation." Desperation is of special concern in the sexual part of life, which is the most intimate focus of man's experience. Intimate, loving communication can help to relieve every person's desperation.

Still, nearly everybody finds it difficult to express love, intimacy, or even concern in words at some time in his life. In sexual matters, however, such expressions count almost as much as physical contact.

No matter what else you do with this book, then, we urge you to find or make ways to communicate your interest, your concern, your love for your partner. Tell your partner that you appreciate and need him or her. If you are a methodical person, you might make a wallet card with the words LOVE, INTIMACY, CONCERN written on it; you can use it to remind yourself to express these all-important feelings.

Throughout our book we remind you that the exercises described in it should be tried only after you and your partner have read them and discussed them. We suggest that you talk over what you have accomplished and what you want to accomplish. In discussing sexuality, talk over not only techniques and behavior, but also feelings of love, intimacy, and concern. It may take work to break down the natural hesitation you may feel, but the benefits to yourself and to your partner will be immeasurable.

While you discuss your sexual experiences, be sure to tell your partner what you like and dislike. One counselor, for instance, reports that many persons want to talk about sexual odors, but that they cannot bring themselves to talk about those subjects. Our culture has so many concerns about cleanliness that sexual partners may deprive themselves of pleasurable experience (or expose themselves to unpleasant experience) for fear of mentioning sexual odors. Breaking out of the cultural restrictions will help you feel more open and cooperative with your partner.

EXPRESSING FEELINGS

How can you express your feelings? Anything you do will of course be an expression of your own personality and your own needs. We can only give you some suggestions; try any of them that seem comfortable and helpful to you.

1. "I need you." This expression is true for the great majority of people. It can be comforting to you yourself to admit need. But the best effect of this statement is that it reinforces the other person's sense of worth. It also opens possibilities for further communication. You can "need" your partner in many ways; it is up to you to tell how.

2. "You make me feel good." This is almost a definition of a good lover. How important it is to tell your partner that he or she can do what is most necessary! Feeling good is not limited to sexual expression, of course. It also includes confidence and appreciation, both of which work both to and from the partners.

3. "I am thinking about you." Expression of thoughtful interest and concern is especially important in times of stress and trouble, but it is always welcome, even in happy times. It is a fact of human behavior that *expressing* concern for another person will lead to genuine concern in fact.

PLANNING EXERCISES

After you have completed the non-genital and genital pleasuring exercises, you should sit down with your partner and discuss what you have learned individually and as a couple. Also talk over where to proceed next. You might decide to work together on improving comfort with oral-genital sex, or perhaps you will simply decide to move on to the non-demand exercises or to the intercourse techniques. You should decide your program according to your own needs rather than proceeding by the order of the book.

In subsequent exercises, we suggest following the same procedure: reading a chapter individually, discussing it as a couple, and then discussing it as a couple by reading an exercise together and deciding when and how to proceed. Obviously you do not want to cease intercourse until you get to the intercourse chapter. However, we suggest that not every exercise end in intercourse. One possibility is to have intercourse at times other than when you are doing the exercises. Another is to complete an exercise, talk about it for five or ten minutes, and then go on to foreplay and intercourse. On other occasions, follow the exercises in such a way that you get the most learning and enjoyment from each one, rather than putting pressure on yourselves to have each experience end in intercourse.

It is our hope that this book will make you aware of and comfortable with a view of sexuality that considers pleasuring, foreplay, intercourse, and afterplay and afterglow flowing in a natural, comfortable way. This is an attitude toward sexuality in which orgasm is the natural culmination of sexual arousal, rather than the ultimate goal for which you are striving. The attitude toward sexuality which we advocate in this book encompasses your whole body, not just your genitals, and includes playful, affectionate touching in the same category as genital stimulation. This kind of attitude expresses a view of sensuality and sexuality that sees you as a person communicating your needs and preferences in a healthy, open way to your partner.

There are chapters you might want to read without going through the exercises. Although you might get some benefit from reading alone, we encourage you to do the exercises where they are appropriate so that you can be comfortable with the new approaches to sexuality. The psychologists talk about good adjustments, psychological and sexual, as being present when the individual's attitudes, feelings, and behavior all go together and reinforce each other. By doing the exercises, you increase the chances to dovetail your sexuality with the other components of positive psychological adjustment.

Reading the exercises should help to modify your attitudes. Doing the exercises (and thereby increasing your skill and comfort) is intended to change your behavior. Finally, being aware of your own reactions and giving and getting feedback from your partner will help to change your feelings. In these many and different ways we hope that you as a couple learn to grow in sexual comfort and pleasure.

2   A Self-Exploration and Enhancement Program for Women

All people are sexual beings, from the day they are born to the day they die. Acceptance and enjoyment of sexuality varies from person to person. For some, sexual feelings develop naturally and at a young age; for others, sexual feelings and the acceptance of sexuality are blocked. Because of cultural factors and personal experiences or expectations, some women may not be as responsive to sex as men.

       The purpose of the exercises in this chapter is to increase your knowledge of and comfort with your body and its natural, healthy reactions. A good way to remove blocks to naturally-occurring sensual and sexual reactions is through a systematic, anxiety-reducing self-exploration of your body and responses. The set of exercises in this chapter is designed to help you do that.

FEMALE ORGASM

Some women are nonorgasmic; in other words, they have not learned to experience the feeling of gradually increasing excitement and responsivity which is followed by a moment of release (orgasm, climax) and accompanied by a great deal of pleasure and warm feelings. But practically all women can experience orgasm.

Orgasm in a woman lasts from three to ten seconds. The orgasm consists of rhythmic muscle contractions followed by the release of muscle tension and the release of blood congestion in the pelvic area. Women may have several orgasms in a row.

The media have over-dramatized the importance of orgasm and the sensations involved. Orgasm is different for each person and different in different situations. It has been described by some as a "pop," where the tension has built up and then gives way and is replaced by a feeling of warmth and enjoyment. Others have compared different kinds of orgasms to waves — one a gentle ripple as opposed to another, a roaring wave in which the person might lose consciousness for a second or two.

Orgasm is a *natural* culmination of sexual feelings and responsivity. An orgasm cannot be willed. The more you concentrate on it and strive for it, the less likely an orgasm will occur. One healthy way to think about orgasm is this: It is a delightful heightening of pleasurable feelings beginning with sensual touching, moving into sexual arousal, and ending with enjoyable touching and afterglow. Before a woman can be orgasmic, she must learn to be comfortable with her own body and her sensual and sexual reactions.

PROCEDURE FOR THIS CHAPTER

We suggest that you first read the entire chapter, and then proceed through the exercises slowly, step-by-step. There are comments as to length of time to spend on each step, but because each person is different, consider these as guidelines rather than inflexible rules. Remember, you are a unique person and only you can know what is most enhancing for yourself.

One of the first steps is to experience comfort with and knowledge of your body. Set aside a time in your day when you will not be interrupted. Decide that this is your time; you will not answer the door or the phone. If you have small children, afternoon nap time is perfect; or when your husband is home, put him in charge of the house and children. Do whatever you can to make this your own time.

Keep three rules in mind:

1. The goals are exploration, learning, and enjoyment rather than the accomplishment of a specific task. There are no right or wrong responses.

2. In terms of time to be spent on this exercise you should be flexible and continue unless you become uncomfortable or anxious. Ideally, one set of exercises should be done per session, and each session should be from thirty to sixty minutes long. However, because there might be some embarrassment and hesitancy at first which might cause you to start and stop quickly, try to have the first sessions at least five minutes long and then gradually, progressively longer.

3. Decide how you feel about your surroundings. Do you want the lights off or on; do you want music on or not; do you like using oil, lotions or powders or not? Decide for yourself and feel free to change.

First Set of Exercises for Chapter 2

You should get to know your body first so you can be comfortable with it. Making sure you will have uninterrupted time and privacy, draw a hot bath and add some of your favorite bath oil. Stretch out in the tub, and oil or soap your body, enjoying the sensation of your hands touching your calves, thighs and arms. Spend some extra time on your toes and feet, massaging them until they are very relaxed.

Feel the softness behind your knees, and on the inside of your upper arms. Cross your arms so opposite hands grasp your waist. Slide your hands across your body and down your sides to rest on your thighs. Sitting up, place your palms together and your knees together. Slide your hands through your thighs and down your legs; caress your ankles. The idea is to feel comfortable, aware of and responsive to all parts of your body. Lie back and relax until you feel ready to continue. Then dry yourself in a slow, comfortable manner, almost caressing yourself dry.

When you have finished, go into your bedroom without clothes on and lie on your bed. You may want to darken your bedroom, cover yourself with a sheet to get warmer, or have music on the radio or stereo. Do what you feel is most natural for you. Make yourself comfortable, using pillows to support yourself in the most relaxing position you can get into. Close your eyes, and concentrate on relaxing. Be aware of any tension in your body. The easiest way to discover and control tension is to tense various muscle groups (arms, legs, back, chest, and face), and then to relax them. To facilitate the relaxation, repeat to yourself expressions like "Relax and feel my body" or "Feel relaxed and calm." Use calm, deep, relaxed and regular breathing to enhance the sensations of relaxation. During a minute or two, each time you inhale, think of the word "relax," and each time you exhale, think of the word "calm."

When you are feeling relaxed and comfortable, cross your arms so that they cross over your navel. Clasp your outside thighs with your hands gently. Curl up slowly and roll to one side. Notice the feelings of touching and movement.

Touching your feet, legs, thighs, stomach, chest, lower back, neck, face, arms, and fingers, try different types of touch — light stroking, patting, heavy massaging, rubbing, and scratching.

Be aware of the sensations that come with the different kinds of touching in the different parts of your body.

When you feel comfortable with touching the non-genital parts of your body, it is time for a visual self-exploration. If possible, you should have a full-length mirror. A valuable visual-exploration technique is to take a piece of cardboard and hold it first in front of one eye and then the other. Notice which parts of your body look different to you. Find at least one part which is different from its other side. Then look at your whole body (front, side, and back views) with both eyes and pick out at least two areas that you find particularly attractive (these do not necessarily have to be sexual areas). Next, either view yourself with a small hand mirror as you lie on the bed, or lie facing a full-length mirror with two pillows propped under your buttocks.

The first important aspect in learning about your genital anatomy is to be able to identify the parts of the vulval area. (See Figure 1) When exploring the genital area, the goal is to be comfortable with the sight and feel of your genitals. Do not worry about sexual arousal. Separate the labia majora with your fingers, looking carefully at the labia minora, and find the clitoris under its hood. Notice how the labia minora surround the vaginal opening. Spread the vaginal opening with two fingers and notice the color and texture of the interior. Feel the warmth, softness and dampness. Insert a finger into your vagina and watch with the mirror. What happens? How does it feel? Touch the mons area, the perineum (the area just forward of the anus), and around the urethera.

When you are satisfied that you know exactly how this part of your body looks, close your eyes. Touch all the areas again, imagining how they look in the mirror. As you relax again, you should be comfortable in feeling that you know more about and feel more positive about your body now than perhaps ever before in your life.

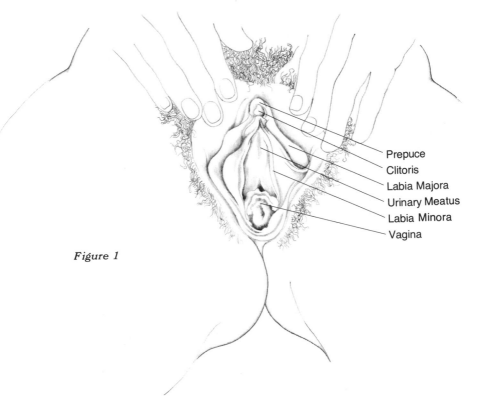

Prepuce
Clitoris
Labia Majora
Urinary Meatus
Labia Minora
Vagina

Figure 1

KEY TO FIGURE 1

1. Mons veneris. A raised area created by a layer of fat over the pubic bone. The *mons* becomes covered with hair at puberty.

2. Labia majora. The literal translation of this Latin term is "greater lips."

3. Labia minora. These folds of sensitive tissue become slightly erect as blood flows into them when a woman is sexually aroused.

4. Prepuce. This hood-like fold of tissue is formed by the joining of the *labia minora*. The prepuce partially covers the clitoris.

5. Clitoris.   This is the most sensitive and responsive of the female genitalia. It becomes slightly enlarged and erect when it is stimulated. The clitoris is the center of response during orgasm.

6. Urinary meatus.   This is the outlet for urine from the bladder, via the urethra.

7. Vagina.   This organ is about four or five inches long. Its walls normally touch each other, but during intercourse they may stretch considerably, and of course they become greatly stretched during childbirth. The vagina receives lubrication from mucus secretions when the woman is sexually aroused. A thin elastic membrane, the *hymen*, partially covers the opening of the vagina; the hymen can be broken or stretched in a number of ways. The outer third of the vagina is ordinarily the most sensitive area, although sensitivity varies from woman to woman. The pubococcygeal muscle is about one finger joint inside the vagina.

Second Set of Exercises, Chapter 2

We suggest beginning your exercises today by taking a good long relaxing bath. Get used to the feeling of caressing your body, and spend some extra time noticing things about it that you may not have noticed before. Exactly where is that mole? What does it feel like to touch it? How does it feel to pat your back gently? How does your stomach feel after you have stopped stroking it?

PURPOSES OF THE BATH

The bath serves two functions: to help you relax and to clean your body. Using a mild soap, gently cleanse your genitals. As you are doing this, gently separate the labia with your fingers and clean the inside of the large labia to remove secretions.

Two highly-charged subjects should be mentioned here. First, whether you keep or cut your body hair is your own business. Some shave; some do not. Make your decision to suit your comfort and taste, not some ideal promoted by the depilatory and razor industries. Second, everybody has odors occasionally. Genital secretions break down into several odor-causing substances. We suggest that you cleanse away such odor-causing secretions, but in doing so we are not suggesting that you give up your humanity to the soap and perfume manufacturers. It is our personal view that genital cleanliness is a sign of consideration for your partner, but many of our readers have objected that, in saying so, we have projected an image of the ideal lover as sanitized and plastic.

As you cleanse your genitals, notice that you can feel the small bump. This is the clitoris. Wash the entire area gently. Take extra time to dry your body, using your favorite type of towel. Some prefer a soft towel and some a stiff type of terrycloth for a stimulating massage while drying.

RELAXING AND SELF-ENHANCING

In the self-enhancement exercises do what you particularly enjoyed previously, but don't hesitate to be inventive. Add your own body caresses as you relax. The focus will be on feeling more comfortable with genital touch. Start by touching your breasts. You will notice that if you slowly move one hand up the opposite side of your body, then over your chest to the breast, the areola will rise. Both in observing and touching your breasts, be aware of which might be larger and more responsive. Notice the difference in feeling when the areola is hard and when soft. Also notice what is the most enjoyable form of breast stimulation for you: stimulating concurrently, touching the areola with just the palm of your hand, rubbing downward on the breast and then pulling back up. Also, remember there are many normal differences among women both in degree and nature of response to stimulation. Some women very much enjoy having their breasts caressed. Others do not. You want to find out about yourself.

While you are relaxing on the bed, curl up on your side and place your hands on the inside of your knees. Slide them slowly up the inside of your legs until they reach your genital area. You may find it very sensual to run your fingers through your pubic hair. Feel the soft skin covering the area between your vagina and your anus. This is the perineum. Be aware of the damp warmth of the labia majora. Separate the lips, and with your fingertips touch and outline the labia minora. Find the clitoris, and placing a finger above it, slide back the clitoral hood. This is a small movement; you may have a hard time identifying it. Trace the outer edge of the vaginal opening with your finger tip. Notice that it is damp, moist, and warm. This normal body secretion is clean and germ-free. It is natural, normal, positive and necessary. It reflects healthy responsiveness. You might want to take a drop of this on your fingertip and put it on your tongue to taste it.

If at any time you feel anxious or uncomfortable, do not stop completely or remove your hand. Just go back a step or two until you feel comfortable and focus on the relaxation and pleasure. Remember, there is no rush; proceed at your own pace. Gradually you will feel more comfortable and enjoy your natural body reactions.

Third Set of Exercises For Chapter 2

Now that you have some knowledge of your body and are able to be relaxed, you will find that you can probably skip some of the steps that were necessary in the beginning. You are probably feeling much more comfortable with your body now than before. You may be discovering that there are special places that feel much better than others. Although you should continue with exploring and learning, the next emphasis is on enhancing specific feelings of pleasure and responsiveness. You have a natural right to feel sensuous and sexual, and to enjoy feelings of pleasure and responsiveness. Bask in your own pleasure and bodily responses.

Feel the freedom of owning every feeling you have. You might try using imagery or fantasy (both sexual and non-sexual) to facilitate your pleasure. All fantasies and thoughts are normal; let your fantasies go. See what kinds of fantasy turn you on, accept them, and utilize them to enhance your enjoyment. You might want to imagine yourself running free and naked on a beach. Visualize a man telling you that you are the best lover he has ever known. Fantasize making love for three hours straight, being stimulated by two lovers at once — anything that you really can tune into. Simply give free reign to your fantasies and imagination, and use them to enhance your sexual pleasure.

PLEASURING THE CLITORAL AREA

Most women find the clitoral area is particularly pleasurable. After some non-genital touching, move your hand to your clitoris and let your finger move across it slowly, back and forth. This can be a very warm and sensuous feeling. As you become aroused, the clitoris becomes larger and withdraws under the clitoral hood. This is your body's way of protecting you from discomfort because direct clitoral stimulation usually causes pain. You can then massage around the clitoral shaft, thereby indirectly stimulating the clitoris. Try to enjoy feelings of warmth, sensuousness, and sexual responsiveness very deeply. Enjoy these exciting feelings as you begin to understand just how your body can respond. If at any time you become anxious or uneasy, relax; move back a step or two and focus on the sense of comfort, not the sense of discomfort or uneasiness.

While massaging the vaginal area and the vagina itself, take the secretion and spread it throughout the vulval area. Then spread the vaginal opening with two fingers and notice the texture of the interior. Feel the warmth and dampness. Insert a finger into your vagina and be aware of the feelings. Move the finger inside the vagina and study the folds of flesh inside. Notice whether there are special places that feel better than any others. You can focus all your attention on touching the vulval area or with one hand you can be massaging the clitoral shaft while you caress a breast with the other hand. Do what allows you the most sensuous and sexual feelings.

Fourth Set of Exercises for Chapter 2

Try to focus on the idea that your body is one integrated being. The whole of you can feel sensuous and sexual. There should no longer be an artificial barrier between touching your genitals and touching the rest of your body. In exploring your body and reactions today, you can facilitate the process by repeating sentences like these to yourself as you relax and explore: "Relax and enjoy my body." "Just let go and feel my body." "Find out what feels good." "Let myself go and feel it all."

During this experience, focus on giving yourself permission to enjoy the sensual and sexual feelings and respond to them. You may be discovering that there are special places that feel much better than others. Notice what they are and give them special attention. You will find that on some days certain things feel particularly good, and some days they don't. So you must find both the things that are a turn-on for you, and also the pattern and rhythm to which you respond best. Many women experiment with different types of stroking (circular, upward, patting, quick touch, teasing, etc.). Also, try variations in pressure to see what is enjoyable for you and what is not. Try stroking your clitoris with one hand while touching your breasts or stomach with the other. Or try slowly massaging the clitoral shaft with one hand and rapidly rubbing the perineum with the other.

You might want to engage in explicit and enjoyable

sexual fantasies, or relaxing fantasies, or anything else which would enhance your experiencing your bodily reactions. You might imagine that the sexiest man you have ever known is making love to you. Imagine yourself being loved in a variety of different situations that you think would be exciting. Try thinking about a favorite love-story passage from a book or poem; it might help you feel maximum sensuousness. Fantasizing is not only normal but quite positive in increasing sexual feelings.

A REMINDER

Remember, the exercises in this book are to help you experience your body in positive, sensual and sexual ways and to increase awareness of the naturalness and healthiness of your responses. At this point, you may or may not be experiencing orgasm — climax, going over the top, popping, or whatever the feeling of physical and emotional release is for you personally. If you are experiencing orgasm, that is fine. You have taken a major step in becoming a more sexually responsive woman. If you are not, do not be discouraged. The exercises so far make up only one step in learning to respond and to accept your responsiveness. If you are more knowledgeable and accepting of your body reactions, you have learned the important concept of this exercise. It is simply a matter of time, practice, feedback, and discovery of the particular feelings and instances that are sensuously powerful enough to carry you along to this point. If you keep working, enjoying and exploring your body, you will indeed achieve a greater sensual and sexual responsivity which will *naturally* culminate in orgasm.

USING A VIBRATOR FOR SELF-ENHANCEMENT

Before you proceed to these exercises, you should have completed the program on a self-exploration and enhancement. Thus you should have a basic knowledge of comfort with your body and its reactions. The use of the vibrator is simply an extension of the previous experiences. Its purpose is to increase the feelings of stimulation.

Some women have reservations about using a vibrator. Perhaps the best way to think of the vibrator is that it is a helpful means to enhance your feelings of sexual response and to understand the sensations of the orgasmic response. Research has shown that for many women orgasmic response with vibrator stimulation is a good first step toward orgasm by self-stimulation first and then to orgasm by partner stimulation and ultimately orgasm through intercourse.

Among the best types of vibrators to use are electric, two-speed, hand-held, self-contained units with several kinds of rubber attachments. They are sold in drug and department stores as muscle, body or scalp massagers. A second type is a facial massage vibrator that straps onto the hand and causes the fingers to vibrate. A third type is a vibrator that is shaped somewhat like a penis; this too is sold as a facial massage vibrator. Use the one you feel the most comfortable with.

When you use a vibrator, you might also wish to use a sterile lubricant jelly to prevent soreness. Before starting the exercises, you should read the operating instructions for the vibrator so you know how to use it and what to expect from it. Each exercise is constructed to be tried in a single short session and then repeated for longer periods. However, consider the exercises simply as guidelines and proceed at your own pace with comfort.*

---

*Most sets of exercises have four steps, except in this chapter, where there are two sets of exercises and therefore eight steps. Each step is somewhat more complex than the one before.

Fifth Set of Exercises For Chapter 2

To begin, you might want to take a relaxing bath. Afterwards, allow yourself to feel comfortable lying on the bed with your body relaxed. Focus your thoughts on your sensuous feelings. You might do some non-genital or genital touching to get yourself more in contact with your bodily feelings without the vibrator. Then turn the vibrator on and hold it in your hands. If it is a two-speed device, notice the different sensations caused by each speed. Then try pressing the vibrator gently against your face, arm, and leg. Get used to the enjoyable sensations that are produced by the vibrator.

After you are feeling comfortable with the vibrator and your body is feeling relaxed and sensual, press the vibrator gently against those areas which you have already found to be very pleasurable. These can be non-genital, genital, or both. Don't pressure yourself for any sexual response; just allow yourself to be relaxed and comfortable.

You can end this exercise when you feel that you have reached the point that you are comfortable with accepting your positive and natural bodily reactions to the sensations of the vibrator. If, however, you experience some discomfort, simply repeat the exercises at another time until you do feel comfortable and then proceed to the remaining exercises. Remember, move at your own pace. This exercise should be a non-pressured learning experience for you.

Sixth Set of Exercises For Chapter 2

Take your time and allow yourself to be relaxed and comfortable before using the vibrator. Begin its use on pleasurable non-genital parts of your body. Next, spreading your knees, begin at the center of your thigh and move the vibrator slowly up your leg until it is resting against the labia majora. Then, spreading the labia with your fingertips, gently lay the vibrator next to the clitoris.

Relax and enjoy the flow of feelings. You already know that these feelings are natural and a healthy part of you, so stay with them and enhance them. If at any time you do become uneasy or anxious because these new feelings might be frightening (or just because they are new), simply go back to relaxing and use the vibrator on non-genital body parts until you again feel comfortable. Then move the vibrator to a sensitive part of your genital area (See Figure 2) and simply relax and be relatively passive while the vibrator provides stimulation. Try to stay passively relaxed as long as it feels comfortable, but try for at least five minutes, lengthening the use of the vibrator every day up to forty-five minutes.

Figure 2

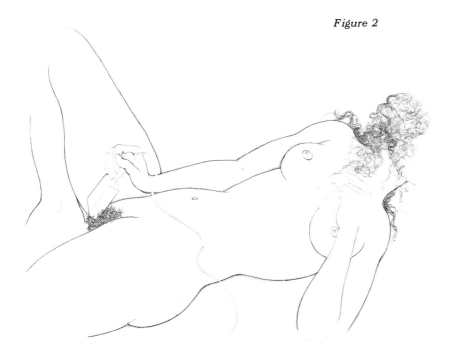

Seventh Set of Exercises For Chapter 2

Begin again with using the vibrator on non-genital areas. Continue to feel your body and to search for new feelings. At this point, you might want to make use of explicit sexual fantasies, either thinking of your partner or thinking of making love to your favorite movie hero; or enjoy any erotic fantasy that turns you on. Your favorite music might provide a comfortable atmosphere. Some people find that reading about sexual encounters in books while using the vibrator enhances their feelings. Some very erotic passages from *Fanny Hill*, from an erotic magazine, or from a favorite love poem might help you feel the maximum sensuousness. Do what is exciting and helpful for you.

Focus the vibrator on the most sensuous and sexual areas of your genital region. For most women this will be the areas around the mons and the clitoral shaft. Hold the vibrator on these areas, massaging at first in slow gentle movements and then more rapidly. Keep the vibrator on the genital area at least ten minutes and then longer periods of time up to forty-five minutes. You might try the vibrator intravaginally, if you have the kind that can be used that way. Insert it when you are feeling very sensuous, and move it about to find special positions that feel better than others. If you have the kind of vibrator in which your fingers are free, insert one or two fingers intravaginally and allow the vibrator to provide pulsating movements to the fingers. Experiment. Try things that will enhance your feelings of sexuality. It is impossible to do this wrong. The important consideration is that it feels good to you. No one can tell you what you enjoy better than you yourself can. You need to learn for yourself what makes you responsive, and then you can share it with your partner. Remember to work at your own speed, continuing to try and to do what feels uniquely right for you.

At this point you will probably be experiencing a physical, sexual, and emotional release — orgasm, climax, popping,

going over the top — which you have been expecting. You can
simply accept these feelings as the natural culmination of your body
exploration. Once you have learned for yourself how to be
responsive and orgasmic, the next step is to share this information
with your partner and to begin working toward a mutually-enjoyable
sex relationship.

Some women, once they learn to be orgasmic with
the vibrator, quickly learn to be orgasmic with their partner's or
their own touch and sometimes then to be orgasmic in intercourse.
Other women take longer to adjust completely to the new feelings
and sensations of their new experience. The fact remains, however,
that once you have become orgasmic, you have taken a major step in
acceptance and enhancement of yourself as a sexual person. Now
with a little time and a cooperative, supportive partner you will
learn to respond more to manual touch and then to penile
stimulation. The following is a series of suggested transition steps.

Eighth Set of Exercises For Chapter 2

You may have been sharing with your partner as you have been
working in the program with the vibrator. Now ask him to join you in
a session. After the usual bath or shower, when you are feeling
relaxed and comfortable, both of you should assume the
non-demand position. (The woman is on her back with the man on
his side next to her, legs bent, so that her legs rest on top of his.)
Separating your feet and legs, apply the vibrator as you usually do,
except that you will want to take your partner's hand and rest it on
top of yours, so that he can follow the movements you make and
share in your pleasure. Talk while doing this, sharing your feelings
with him. Ask him to share his feelings with you. Allow yourself to
feel aroused and to be orgasmic. Doing so allows you to feel
comfortable being orgasmic in your partner's presence. Also, if you
allow yourself to be orgasmic, you will provide an excellent learning

experience for your partner in understanding what techniques of genital stimulation are effective and pleasurable to you.

When you and your partner are both comfortable with the vibrator procedure, let him use the vibrator with your hand on his. Then begin to alternate his manual caresses with vibrator caresses, until more and more of the time is spend with his hand alone. Once you have begun to respond easily and naturally to your partner's manual stimulation, you will be able to be orgasmic without using the vibrator. To enhance the transition, try to get your breathing in rhythm with your partner's breathing, and tell him how you are feeling. See Chapter 1, "Communication," page 10.

AFTERWORD

The most important part of your response is to stay with the feelings your body has; to respond to your feelings about your partner; and to share with him. Share in both giving and taking pleasure. As he caresses you, use your hands to tell him how you feel by caressing him and sharing your pleasure and sexuality.

Once you are comfortable in achieving orgasm by both vibrator and manual stimulation, you will be feeling more nearly sure of yourself as a woman, and you will be pleased with your acceptance of your sexuality. At this point, you might want to move on to the exercises to increase vaginal feeling and response and the exercises to increase arousal for women. See Chapter 6.

3 A Self-Exploration and Enhancement Program for Men

The physique and genital size of the male body have been highly valued among men. Being proud and aware of his own body can be beneficial to a male. On the other hand, males' feelings about their bodies can have some significant negative aspects. Foremost among these negative aspects are (1) a common emphasis on penis size as an indication of virility; (2) emphasis of the importance of sexual functioning ability*; and (3) the overemphasis on sexual feeling by the female and downplaying or totally ignoring sensual feelings by the male.

CULTURAL PRESSURES ON MEN
Our culture encourages males (much more so than females) to develop positive attitudes toward their bodies and sexual functioning. However, with regard to sex as elsewhere, competition

---

*This emphasis can be seen in the sexual Superman myth, which says that a male should be able to get an erection and to perform sexually with anybody — anywhere and at anytime.

has been overemphasized, with the result that sexual *performance* is stressed as the most important, if not the only, criterion of masculinity. Males commonly learn to value vigorous competition, strength, and rapid sexual performance more than slow, gentle, flowing movement and sensuous touching. They may even consider sensuality as not masculine. Males may seem out of touch with sensual sensitivity to themselves and their bodies. Consequently, they are also out of touch with their partners' sensitivity too. Not only does insensitivity prevent a male from enjoying his own sexual and sensual responses, but it also makes it more difficult to understand, accept, and enjoy female sexual and sensual response. To acquire sensual feelings and an appreciation of sensuality apart from the demands of sexual performance, the male must nurture a new awareness of himself and his body — that is, an awareness of himself as a sensual and sexual person.

Everyone — male or female — is sensual and sexual simply because he or she has a body. Being a sexual and sensual human should be accepted as natural and good.

Many men too often isolate their sexuality from themselves as persons. Then they see sex merely as a means of release for a physical need, an act whose performance proves their masculinity, or as a weakness in women to be exploited in order to conquer them. Instead, they should consider sex as an integral part of both males and females. To develop a positive awareness of sexuality and perhaps to change any negative, performance-based feelings, you need to develop comfort with your own body and your sensual and sexual reactions. Once you know your body and are comfortable with it, you can share it with your partner more easily.

One way to remove inhibitions to naturally-occurring sensual and sexual reactions is through a systematic self-exploration of your body. A first step in the process of understanding and accepting your sexuality is to develop your knowledge of your body and to experience comfort with your bodily reactions. You should keep three things in mind while doing these exercises. First, the idea is to facilitate exploration, learning, and enjoyment rather than to accomplish a task. Activities should be non-demanding and non-goal-oriented. There are no right or wrong responses. Second, be flexible in the amount of time spent on each exercise; take the exercises slowly and at your own pace. As a general, broad guideline you might be spending thirty minutes to an hour on each exercise.

Typically, males seldom touch themselves except in goal-oriented masturbation, where the quick release of sexual tension in ejaculation (orgasm) is emphasized. The desire for a quick orgasm keeps the male from understanding his body as a whole, and himself as a sexual and sensual being. When a male has only touched himself to masturbate, it is difficult for him to appreciate non-demanding, non-goal-oriented touching and exploration.

For the male who wishes to increase his awareness of himself as a sensual and sexual person, the exercises that follow are intended to serve as a beginning to help increase body knowledge and awareness. If at any point in the exercises you become hesitant, tense or embarrassed, simply go back a step or two and relax until you feel comfortable again. Remember, this is some you are doing for yourself. Move at your pace.

Third, although at some time or other in their lives, approximately 96% of all males masturbate, the feeling remains that masturbation is somehow abnormal or perverted. In fact, masturbation is perfectly normal and natural, and it is a positive aspect of sexual development. There is no reason to feel guilty about it. Self-exploration and masturbation are the best ways to learn about and enhance your feelings about your body and your sexuality. They can enhance rather than inhibit later sexual relations with a partner when you guide and share with your partner what you've learned about yourself. Self-exploration and masturbation are beneficial, legitimate modes of sexual expression in adults — single and married — and research indicates that a majority of married males employ masturbation as a sexual expression at least occasionally.

First Set of Exercises for Chapter 3

You might begin with a hot bath or shower. Soap your body in a leisurely fashion, gently massaging at first and then more vigorously kneading your larger muscle groups: arms, shoulders, neck, back, thighs, calves, and feet. Spend extra time on your toes and feet. Massage them until they are very relaxed. Be aware of the degree of muscle tension in each body part. Healthy muscle has some normal tension (muscle *tonus*) that is natural, but muscle *tonus* does not prevent one from feeling relaxed. Nervous tension from the everyday anxiety of life can tense muscle groups, producing an uncomfortable, tight feeling.

Allow any anxiety or tension to drain from your body and replace it with a feeling of calmness and relaxation by just letting go and allowing the muscles to relax. Be aware of the physical feelings of warmth, heaviness, and comfort and the psychological feelings of calm, confidence, and control.

The coarser spray of a shower gives a good massage, and you can just soak in the warmth and moisture. Turn your face into the spray. It can massage and relax the muscles of your face. Then bow your head and let the water run over your head, face, and neck. Let your worries, concerns or embarrassments drain from you so that you can respond spontaneously to the positive sensations of your own body. Learning how to feel relaxed and comfortable may take some effort in the beginning, but focus your energies on your bodily sensations, being aware of them and facilitating them so that you become relaxed. This is your time — enjoy it!

When you are feeling clean, relaxed, and comfortable — not when you *think* you *should be* feeling that way — get out of the shower and enjoy the feeling of your wet, dripping body. Notice the cooling sensation of water evaporating from your skin. As you dry yourself, use the towel to give yourself a comfortable massage.

Rather than putting on clothes, simply go to your bedroom in the nude and sprawl on your bed in the most comfortable position you can get into. Be sure that your bedroom is warm enough so that you won't be cold without any clothes on. Keep the room as comfortable as possible for yourself. Do what you prefer; put your favorite music on the stereo and darken the room if you wish.

Settle back on the bed, close your eyes and just think about relaxing. Be aware of your body and where it may be tense. The easiest way to discover tension is to tense or tighten various muscle groups (arms, legs, back, chest, face) and then to release the tension and prolong the relaxed feeling that follows by focusing on it and letting your muscles relax even more. To facilitate and enhance feelings of relaxation, breathe deeply and regularly for one or two minutes: each time you inhale, think the word "relax." Each time you exhale, think the word "calm." You might also repeat to yourself phrases like "relax and feel my body," "let go completely," "relax more and more, deeper and deeper . . . ."

When you are feeling relaxed and comfortable, double up in a ball and roll to one side. As you roll, notice the feelings of your body as you move and touch yourself. Begin slowly and gently touching yourself, first touching only the non-genital parts of your body. Touch your feet, legs, thighs, stomach, chest, lower back, neck, face, arms, and your fingers. Experiment with and be aware of different sensations from light stroking, rubbing, gentle patting, light touching, and heavy massage. Now change your position and really let your body stretch out. Straighten and stretch your arms and legs. Then stiffen your whole body, and then allow it to relax. Repeat the non-genital touching in this position, and be aware of your feelings and experiences.

Now that you are aware of some of your body's sensations, and you are aware of touching your body, you might do some visual exploration. Look at yourself in a mirror (a full-length mirror is preferable). Take a piece of cardboard or paper and place it in front of one eye (or simply close one eye). Examine half of your body, then switch; cover your other eye and examine the other half of your body. Find at least one part of your body that does not look the same on both sides. Then look at your whole body (front, side, and back views) with both eyes and pick out at least two nongenital areas that you particularly like.

So far, we have emphasized non-genital touching and looking because males put undue emphasis on their genital anatomy. Now, however, focus on learning about and identifying your genital anatomy. In exploring your genital area, the idea is to be comfortable with the sight and feel of your genitals rather than worrying about sexual arousal. Be aware of and touch the glans of the penis, the coronal ridge, and the sides of the penile shaft. Then examine your scrotum and discover which testis is larger (See Figure 3) Notice how one testis is lower than the other, and be aware of the sensitivity of the scrotal sac. Observe the placement and feeling of your genitals while standing up, while sitting, and while lying down. Once you think that you are aware of your genitals, close your eyes and touch all the areas again, imagining how they look. Then just allow yourself to relax again, and be aware of what part of your body feels most comfortable and most relaxed. End the exercise when you feel that you know more about and feel more comfortable with your own body.

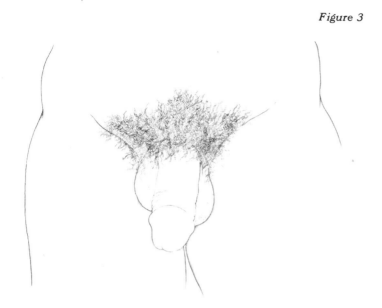

Second Set of Exercises for Chapter 3

Now that you have a basic knowledge of your body, begin to increase your awareness of your sensual and sexual feelings. Again, begin with a shower or bath; this has the twofold purpose of cleaning your body and helping you relax. While you are showering or bathing, be aware of the hair on your body. What places are hairy and which are hairless? Be aware of your beard and how it feels as you touch it. Notice particularly the hair in your armpit and pubic area, and be sure to wash these carefully. Some body secretions and odors can be highly sensuous and sexually arousing; however, body odor caused by not washing might not be attractive to you or to others. Smell the natural scent of your body and think what scents you consider pleasant and positive. If you use deodorant, talc, cologne, or other products on your body, be aware of their scent and feelings.

Go into your bedroom with no clothes on and make yourself comfortable. Begin touching yourself and use the kind of touch that you find most sensuous. Touch the parts of your body that feel best. You might want to experiment with touching your breasts. Some men find breast stimulation very enjoyable and arousing while others get no particular sensations. Watch your nipples and notice the difference when they are soft and flaccid; also note how they become more erect and harder when you massage them. Be aware of your reactions to this experience.

Lying on the bed, place your hands on the insides of your knees and slide them upward along the inside of your thighs, noticing the changes in sensitivity to touch as you approach your genital area. As you do this, notice that the hair on your legs thins out until the front of your upper thighs is nearly hairless as far as your pubic hair. Enjoy the feeling of running your fingers through your pubic hair. Touch and massage the soft skin that covers the area between your genitals and anus; this area is called the *perineum*. It can be a very sensual area.

If at any time you feel anxious or uncomfortable in doing this self-stimulation, don't stop completely or remove your hand. Rather, simply move your hand to a part of the body where you feel more comfortable. The idea is not to avoid the body exploration, but to move back a step or two until you feel comfortable. Remember to take your time and to move at your own pace. This is meant to be an exploring and learning experience; do not put pressure on yourself or feel you must be sexual. Rather, the idea is to increase your awareness of your natural body reactions and to be comfortable with them. In that way, you will be better able to share with your partner.

Now move your hand to your genitals. Discover what type of penile touch is most enjoyable and arousing. Experiment with different types of genital touching; touch your penis using two fingers around the glans, putting your hand around the shaft and stroking it, one hand touching your testicles and the other massaging the frenulum (the fold of skin connecting the penis and scrotum), or do any other type of stimulation you enjoy. If you want to carry this out to ejaculation, you can, but don't feel any pressure to do so. Instead, focus on learning the kind of genital touching that you find arousing. Be aware of the different feelings you have in touching your flaccid penis and your erect penis. Continue this until you feel comfortable with your knowledge of genital stimulation.

Third Set of Exercises for Chapter 3

Now that you feel more comfortable with the natural and healthy sensual and sexual reactions of your body, you can focus on specific feelings of pleasure and responsivity. In order to guide your partner and teach her about what causes you to feel aroused, you must learn that for yourself. You can decide whether or not to shower or bathe before the exercise. When in your bedroom make it as comfortable as you can in terms of the lighting, music, and general atmosphere. To increase feelings of arousal, do not hesitate to use written or visual materials. Many men find their arousal increased by reading erotic or suggestive novels like *Lolita*, or by looking at pictures from *Playboy* or *Penthouse*, or by reading love poems or reading pornography, or by reading letters from their partners. Experiment and see what is most arousing for you. Remember, there are no right or wrong, normal or abnormal methods of stimulation; rather, what feels arousing and sexual for you is good.

Many males find that fantasizing greatly increases their feelings of arousal. Sometimes they fantasize having intercourse with a partner or spouse, sometimes with a movie star.

Many people have their own unique sex fantasies. Feel free to employ the fantasies that arouse you. Don't worry about their content; there is a lot of difference between fantasy and behavior. There is no such thing as an abnormal or bizarre thought or fantasy.

Begin the touching, focusing on comfortable, sensual feelings. A major trap males fall into is making self-stimulation a rapid, strictly genitally-oriented experience. Integrate the sensual and sexual feelings, and enjoy and enhance the resulting sexual arousal. Notice the feelings in your genital area and whole body as your arousal increases. Focus on the type of stimulation which will increase your arousal and allow you to be orgasmic (i.e., have an ejaculation). This might be a slow but gradually increasing movement of your hand along the shaft of the penis, or rubbing the area around the frenulum and tip (glans area) of the penis. Or perhaps you might have one hand massaging the scrotum and the fingers on the other hand manipulating the head of the penis. Do what is most arousing for you.

If and when you ejaculate, be aware of the pleasurable feelings, the feelings of sexual release, and your acceptance of the sexual arousal cycle of your body. Become aware of your own semen, and be accepting of that also. You might want to look at it carefully, touch it, and perhaps even taste it. Again, be aware that it is a natural and positive aspect of you. Allow yourself to bask in the good and natural feelings of your body and your sexual responsivity.

Fourth Set of Exercises for Chapter 3

At this point, your sense of comfort with your body and your sexual responsivity should be developing. To continue this development, this set of exercises is oriented toward continuing to integrate the sensual touching and sexual, genital touching that is most enjoyable and arousing. Also, you might experiment with different techniques of self-stimulation to make yourself aware of the variety of experiences available to you. However, don't fall into the trap of making your touching completely genitally-oriented or completely orgasm-oriented.

Be sure to use the techniques that are most enhancing for you to be in a sensual and sexual mood: music, reading material, relaxation, physical set-up of your bedroom, etc. Begin with sensual, whole-body touch before focusing on your genitals and penis. Maybe you would like to experiment with a lotion or cream to increase sensual and sexual feelings. As you are doing this, feel free to use the kind of fantasies you have found to be the most sexually arousing.

Rather than simply using touch as the only self-stimulation, you might want to try a different means of sexual arousal. Turn over, and rub your penis against the sheets of the bed, perhaps against a blanket between your legs, or against a pillow. You can also feel the sensations of these objects on other parts of your body such as your thighs, buttocks, lower part of your back, chest, etc. Allow yourself to feel your entire body as you continue to feel and increasingly to enjoy the feelings in your scrotum and penis. Discover the kind and amount of pressure you enjoy on your genitals. Constant stimulation is often very arousing, and it adds to the building of the urge to ejaculate. Allow yourself to experiment with and experience the different types of stroking and massaging against your penis (circular, patting, heavy touch, light touch, etc.) and discover for yourself what is most arousing. In this exercise, really let yourself go and experience the maximum in sensuality and sexuality as you experience the healthy arousal and response of your own body.

AFTERWORD

The idea of these exercises is to allow you to experience your body in positive sensual and sexual ways. You should now be comfortable with your whole body and its natural and healthy responsiveness, rather than focused only on your penis and the mere three to ten seconds of orgasm. Now that you feel more comfortable with your body and sensual responses, it will be easier to share this comfort with your partner. In transferring your knowledge of yourself to interacting with your partner, you will probably find that a mixture of sensual non-genital touching and sexual genital touching is most enjoyable and arousing. Also, you will probably find that goal-oriented sexual experiences are generally less fulfilling than non-demanding, mutually arousing experiences that naturally flow into and culminate in orgasm. You have taken the first step toward experiencing yourself and your partner, and toward learning to understand and accept your own and your partner's sexuality.

Pleasuring Using Non-Genital Touching

Couples who have been having sexual intercourse for a while often report that it has become quite routine and standard. The emphasis is usually on intercourse itself and quickly achieving sexual satisfaction. Often, the couple will think back to their first sexual experiences and remember the feelings of excitement, spontaneity, and seductive touching. They wonder what has been lost. What has happened is that intercourse has overshadowed the sense of pleasurable touching, the feelings of sensuality, and a broader-ranging sexuality. The enjoyment of sexuality has been replaced by the emphasis on all touching being oriented toward intercourse. The fun and spontaneity have gone out of sex; they have been replaced by a rigid goal orientation which puts pressure on the individual and the couple to make each sex experience perfect.

The concept behind our non-genital touching and pleasuring exercises is to reorient your attitudes and feelings to more pleasurable and sensual feelings about your body, your partner's body, and your sexuality. The emphasis will be on discovering in a relaxed, non-goal-oriented situation the sensual pleasure you can derive from touching and being touched. Also, and perhaps most important, it allows you to discover for yourself and with your partner what style of touching, stroking, and caressing feel most comfortable and enjoyable. Couples often assume a lot, fall into ruts, and feel uncomfortable about asking their partners for different types of stimulation. These exercises are oriented toward making you comfortable with touching, discovering, and sharing this with your partner with as little demand toward performance or goal-orientation as possible.

We suggest that you first read this chapter through alone, and then talk to your partner about it. Remember, these are suggestions and flexible guidelines rather than rigid rules. The purpose is to explore and experience. You are doing it for yourself because you want to be able to feel like a normal and healthy sensual and sexual person and accept yourself as one. Once you can do this, you will be better able to focus on your partner and appreciate his or her feelings, needs, and sensitivities.

Time and privacy are often problems. We feel that it is of great importance that you are not worried about external factors such as the phone ringing, people coming over, the children walking in, etc. Therefore, plan a time, at least half an hour, when you won't be disturbed — perhaps while the children are asleep or occupied with a babysitter. Take the phone off the hook. Each set of exercises will take from forty-five to ninety minutes; however, this can be flexible depending on your feelings. The exercises have been developed to allow you to proceed in a comfortable, step-by-step fashion, enjoying one thing before moving on to the next. The most important factor is your feeling relaxed and comfortable so that you can explore, discover, and enjoy your feelings of sensuality.

Before beginning an exercise, we suggest that you might bathe or shower together, at least for the first two or three exercises. We suggest this for two reasons: first, it will serve to relax you and enhance comfortable feelings about your body and, second, the issue of proper care and cleanliness of the body can be important in enhancing feelings of sensuality and sexuality.

At this point we should mention the subject of "No." Suppose that one partner suggests sexual activity and the other partner does not want it. The partner who is denied may feel rejected and may avoid further contact if his suggestion is met with a plain no, whether the denial is strongly made or not. Rather than simply saying no, remember to give an alternative.

This principle applies to all sexual activity. Rather than saying no outright to any kind of sexual contact, try suggesting a substitute that would be acceptable to you. You might say, "No, I don't want to have intercourse now, but I would like to have my back rubbed or my legs stroked." Doing so keeps the sexual dialogue open. It also allows the denying partner to suggest, through his statement, that although one kind of activity does not appeal to him, another kind might appeal; he is still ready and willing for sensual or sexual contact of some kind.

Let us remind you that communication lies at the heart of all satisfying sexual experience. If one partner bids for a kind of activity with love and consideration, and the other partner responds with love and consideration, expressing his or her feelings clearly and completely, the exchange of messages alone can be reinforcing and encouraging to both partners.

Most people find some things about appearance important to them. Find out your partner's preferences. Many people fall into the trap of not being aware of their appearance, especially if they are alone with their partner. They fail to fix their hair; they do not wear fresh clothing or watch their weight. For some partners, carelessness can really detract from sexual feelings.

For others, however, the trap can be always being dressed up, being so fastidious that you lose your natural attractiveness. Obviously, humans vary in what they find attractive or sensual, so it is important first to be aware of your own needs and feelings, and then to learn your partner's preferences concerning what is attractive and important to her or him.

First Set of Exercises for Chapter 4

Before beginning you might want to sit and talk with your partner for fifteen minutes, perhaps over a drink or cup of coffee, so that you are feeling relaxed and comfortable. You might want to recall a particular activity or experience where you felt very close to and good about your partner. Express this feeling of tenderness to your partner. While sitting you might put your hands palms down on the table. Ask your partner to do the same, and allow your hands to be caressed. Notice the difference in size and texture between your hands. Much can be communicated by hands touching.

If you shower as a prelude to the pleasuring, you might experiment with different types of spray or temperature; if bathing, try a new type of bath oil or soap. This may increase your awareness of different types of sensual stimuli. Start by soaping your partner's back well, and caressing it as you do so. Trace the muscles and contours you notice and gently rub and massage. Ask your partner to face you. Soap the front of the neck and chest, but at this point go around the breasts. Touch especially the hollows of the neck, the soft area below the ribs and the navel. Move downward to the hips, bypassing the genital area. You should wash your own genital area. Soap the legs while talking to your partner about how it feels. Let your partner soap you in the same manner. Be sure to tell your partner what feels particularly sensuous.

When you have finished, step from the shower or bath and dry each other off, except for the genitals. Take your time in this; slowness and tenderness are important here also. When you're both dry, stand still for a moment and take a good look at your partner. Look at him or her as if he or she were a new person. Notice the one or two things you find particularly attractive and share them with your partner. Then you might walk toward each other, extending your hands and holding your partner's hands. Slide your partner's arms around your waist and stand still and enjoy your partner's arms around your waist and enjoy the closeness of each other. Feel and talk about a new intimacy, warmth, and closeness.

Then go into your bedroom feeling comfortable and natural being in the nude. If you don't feel comfortable walking through the house nude, you can put on a robe or towel, but drop it to the floor as you reach the bedroom, since the pleasuring should be done in the nude. Later, you can feel free to vary the amount of clothing, but first you should learn to be comfortable with your own and your partner's nudity. The room should be at a comfortable, warm temperature; there should be at least a moderate amount of light, but you can partially darken the room if that will make you more comfortable. If you would like it, put your favorite music on the stereo.

One of you will be designated the "pleasurer" and the other the "pleasuree." Typically, you will switch roles during the middle of the exercise, though some people do one session as "pleasurer" and the next as "pleasuree." However, make sure that each partner has an opportunity to do both, since a mutually satisfying relationship requires the comfort of both partners in receiving and giving. Interestingly, most people find it harder to receive (be pleasuree) than to give (be pleasurer). The terms "pleasurer" and "pleasuree" carry no connotations of dominance and submission or femininity and masculinity.

The pleasuree has three tasks. The first is to be passive and only to receive pleasure. The second is to keep his or her eyes closed throughout the first exercise. This accomplishes two things: First, it allows one to concentrate on one's own feelings. Second, and probably more important since your partner might feel awkward doing this for the first time, he will feel less self-conscious if no one is observing. The third task of the pleasuree is to be aware of what parts of his or her body and what types of touch are relaxing, sensuous, or sexual by arousing. In other words, be in touch with your own body and its natural sensual and sexual feelings and responses.

For this first exercise the male is pleasurer and the female pleasuree.

The pleasurer is to learn how to view his partner in a very different way and to feel comfortable giving different types of touch and body stimulation. The pleasuree will begin by lying on her stomach, feeling as receptive, relaxed, and comfortable as possible. The male should first examine his partner from the top of her head to the bottoms of her feet.

During this phase of the exercise the emphasis will be on communication by touch rather than verbally, so both should be silent as much as possible.

Begin by massaging her shoulder muscles. Gently massage the shoulders, being careful not to squeeze the upper neck muscles. Rub gently with the entire hand, moving slowly down the back and sides, being sure to avoid any sudden movements. Be aware of what you see about her body that you find appealing and that you have not noticed before — freckles, tiny scars, muscle indentations, etc. When you reach the waist place your thumbs together, spread your fingers and press and knead gently, caressing the sides and lower back. Then move back up to the head, and either give a scalp massage or just gently run your fingers through her hair. Next, go to the back but this time press down vigorously and give a backrub. Then perhaps you would like to run your fingers over your partner's back in a playful, disorganized manner. If you want to, you can trace special little features of your partner's back with only your fingertips.

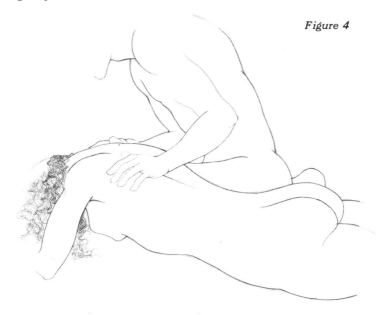

Figure 4

The task of the pleasurer is to do all kinds of things to give the pleasuree a variety of experiences so that she can learn what it is that makes her feel sensual and sexual. The pleasurer will be enjoying trying out various types of touching and really experiencing his partner's body in a new way. The emphasis is on exploring and enjoying, rather than having to prove oneself sexually. Remember, these exercises are guidelines: feel free to explore and to innovate. Be spontaneous.

In continuing your exploring and touching, hold your partner's feet and caress them with your hands. Notice the length of the toes, the texture of the nails. Place your palm so that it covers the arch, and curl your fingers over the top of the foot. Notice the heel as you rub the palm of your hand against it. Outline the division between the top and bottom of the foot with your fingertips. Holding one foot in your hand, caress the top of the foot with your fingers, tracing the valleys between the toes. Gently massage the top of the foot up to the ankle. Moving up that same leg, hold the ankle in your hand while exploring it with the other hand. Gently and slowly move up the calf, caressing and massaging to help your partner relax even more. Pay special attention to rubbing the soft area behind the knee gently. Examine and explore the thigh; look for little places you haven't been familiar with before. Then move up to the buttocks area and massage both buttocks simultaneously. Some people feel negative about this area because of the association with defecation. However, for many people it is one of the most sensuous areas of the body. Touch in a manner that will bring out the enjoyment and sensuousness.

When you are finished with the backside, switch roles of pleasurer and pleasuree and repeat the same sequences. There are large individual differences among people in the time they wish to spend on this part of the exercise, but typically it's between ten and thirty minutes per person. The goals are to explore, to enjoy the touching, to learn about your responses, and to feel comfortable and sensuous. The key words are "slow" and "tender."

After this exercise is completed, sit over a drink or a cup of coffee, discuss the experience and share your feelings. Because talking tends to isolate you from your bodily feelings, it is best to do the exercise in silence. However, afterward we strongly encourage sharing your feelings and reactions in a direct, open manner. (See Chapter 1.)

Second Set of Exercises for Chapter 4

Again begin by taking a bath or shower. Make it even a more relaxed, comfortable, and sensuous experience than the first time by doing the things that are particularly enjoyable to you. Dry your partner off as you did before, commenting and sharing as you do. Then have your partner dry you off, and accept his or her attention. For this set of exercises the female should begin as pleasurer, with the male as pleasuree. In that way she will become more comfortable with initiating contact, as well as being accustomed to giving and receiving affection with ease. When the male is lying on his stomach he should have his eyes open, and since he has some feeling about the area and type of stimulation he finds most pleasing, he will be guiding his partner this time.

Put your hand over your partner's hands to guide them to certain areas of your body. This can be difficult in this position, so feel free to use verbal feedback and guidance as well as touch. Try to find at least two parts of the back of your body that are particularly sensuous. The pleasurer will be learning more about her partner's preferences and will follow his lead. Also, at this point you will be using kissing and other forms of oral contact to stimulate your partner's back. This can include kissing the back of the neck, rubbing the tongue from the top to the bottom of the spinal cord, blowing in the ear and then flicking the tongue in and out, taking gentle "love bites" at various parts of the legs. Remember, different people like different things, and neither you nor your partner knows what he likes until you try it. Remember, there are no right or wrong responses.

When the pleasurer feels she understands her partner's back-pleasuring preferences, she should gently help her partner turn over on his back. The pleasuree should then shut his eyes, relax, and again assume a more passive and receptive attitude. Quite commonly males are not used to the passive role, but it is important that he be passive and receptive so he can learn what sensual feelings he is most responsive to. The pleasurer should first examine the front of the body visually, and notice what parts look particularly attractive.

In touching, be sure to begin with the hands. Cover your partner's hand with yours, and notice the differences in size and texture. Gently massage the fingers, and run your fingertips along the palm. Slide your fingers down the hand, and look for things you have not noticed before. Trace the knuckles and the small lines on the fingers with a fingertip. Gently kiss the soft inner palm of each hand. Gently caress your partner's forearms, one at a time. Notice the softness of the skin on the inner side of the arm. Trace the elbow with your fingers. Placing your thumb in the bend, grasp the forearm, and slide your hand down to the wrist. Then caress both of the arms in their entirety.

You might then want to switch focus and gently explore your partner's face. Notice the feeling of relaxation and comfort on your partner's face; be aware of the difference between this expression and tense expressions you might have noticed in the past. To enhance the feeling of relaxation and sensuousness, very gently massage the forehead, then from the cheeks to the chin, and finally with the fingertips outline your favorite facial features. You might want to kiss your partner's closed eyes gently. In fact, you might want to kiss all the parts of his face.

You might want to massage around his nipples and see if gently touching them feels sensuous or erotic. Many males are erotically sensitive in this area, but they inhibit their natural responses because they think males aren't supposed to feel good there. When you're exploring the chest area use smooth, tender strokes covering not only the chest, but also the sides. Notice the feel of the hair on your hands. Move up to one armpit, and run your hands over it. How does it feel to touch your partner's navel? What about running your hands sideways around the stomach area? Be aware of how the stomach muscles react to your touch. At this point, avoid the genital area, but spend time exploring what type of touch is most sensuous on the inner thighs.

It may happen that sometime at this point or elsewhere in the exercises you might feel very aroused. The male may get an erection or the female may lubricate vaginally. If this happens simply accept it as a natural, sensual, and sexual response. If it does not happen, that is fine, since the idea is to explore and learn. Non-genital pleasuring is not to be a pressured experience to achieve sexual arousal.

Now move down to exploring the front of the legs and feet. In ending this experience, visually re-examine the front of your partner's body, and retouch the two or three areas which you find most attractive. Remember there are no right or wrong areas: Perceptions of attractiveness vary among people. It could be the eyes, the neck, the armpits, the inner thighs — whatever is appealing or arousing to you personally.

Then switch roles of pleasurer and pleasuree, and do the same exercises. However, for this set of exercises the male should not touch or caress his partner's breasts. You will find that each person does the touching and pleasuring differently, which is good because you are learning to be comfortable with your own unique style of giving and receiving pleasure. Afterward, spend time discussing the differences between your style and your partner's, and talk openly about how you can utilize these differences to make your sexual relationship more mutually satisfying.

Third Set of Exercises for Chapter 4

Before beginning today you might sit across from your partner, separated by a table. Make sure it is narrow enough so that by sitting close you can reach your partner's face easily.

Put your hands palms down on the table. Ask your partner to do the same, and to let you caress his or her hands. Move slowly across the table with both hands and cover your partner's hands with yours. Grasp them gently and lift them from the table.

Slide your hands underneath, so that they support the others.
Releasing one hand, cover the other so that it is enclosed within
yours. Lift the hand to your face and rub the back of it on your
cheeks, one then the other. Make eye contact with your partner as
you do this. Then do it again with your eyes closed.

Pick up both hands and place them on your face so
that they enclose it, from your cheeks to your chin. Close your eyes
and slowly move your face from side to side. Holding the wrists,
bend your neck forward, inclining your face toward your chest, and
move the hands to the sides of your neck, eyes closed. Then raise
your face, bring the hands together under the chin, and separate
them so that they slide up your face, stopping as the fingertips reach
your eyes. Turn your face from side to side, and gently kiss the soft
inner palm of each hand. Make eye contact with your partner and
tell with your eyes how you are feeling about the closeness.

Placing the hands on the table once again, imagine
that you will never be allowed to touch them again. Think of what a
void that would leave in your life. How would you touch these hands
if it were the last time — touch, squeeze, kiss them as if it were the
last time? Verbally share your feelings about this experience and
your sense of commitment and caring for your partner.

At this point you can either take a shower or bath, or
if you prefer, go directly to the pleasuring exercises. In the
pleasuring exercises the emphasis will be on guiding your partner
and teaching him or her what feels particularly sensuous and good
on the front part of your body. This time begin with the male as
pleasurer. You will be keeping your eyes open for most of the time so
that you learn to communicate feelings by eye contact. Most of the
guiding will be non-verbal, using your hand over your partner's to
show him what kind of touch and where on your body the feelings
are particularly good for you. To enhance the experience, we
suggest that you use a lotion while massaging. People enjoy several
lotions, including Revlon Wild Lemon, Jergens Hand Lotion,

Johnson's Baby Oil, or any lotion that you particularly like. It might
be fun to go shopping together and pick out one or two lotions you
would like to try. In using lotions, it is important to have them
readily available so you don't have to stop massaging to get the
lotion. If possible, have the lotion heated. Having cold lotion
poured on bare skin can get anyone out of a sensuous mood. If the
lotion is not heated, simply leave one hand on your partner's body
and pour the lotion onto the back of that hand. When it is warmer,
put it on your partner's body.

In doing the non-genital touch, be aware of the
breathing of your partner. See if you can find the rhythmic motion of
the breathing and follow it with the caressing motions of your hands.
Be especially aware of the effect of kissing or rubbing your tongue or
lips around parts of your partner's body. Continue until you and
your partner feel you have a good notion of at least two areas where
touch is particularly sensuous. Then switch roles of pleasurer and
pleasuree, and in your own unique way do your exploration and
learning.

Figure 5

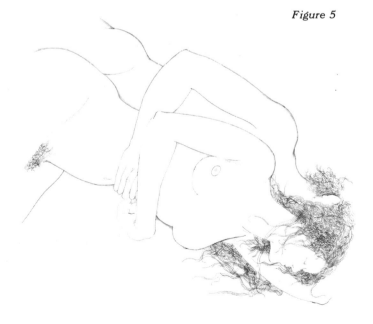

In ending this experience, lie with the male facing the female's back, bodies touching.

If you feel like it, have the male put his arms gently around the female's waist. (See Figure 5) Talk and share the feelings and experience. Then lie quietly until sleep overtakes you.

Fourth Set of Exercises for Chapter 4

You can decide whether or not to shower or bathe. If you decide not to, be sure that your cleanliness is acceptable to you and your partner. We would suggest using a different lotion this time so that your awareness of different smells and sensuous feelings will be enhanced. The emphasis this time will not be on pleasurer and pleasuree. Instead, allow yourselves an increased amount of mutuality and spontaneity. Both partners can more naturally initiate touching and exchange feelings; they can mutually caress each other. In this way, your previous learning about yourself and your partner will transfer more naturally into a mutually satisfying foreplay and pleasuring pattern. However, the touching and pleasuring should still be non-genital.

Also, at this point you will be utilizing some two-way sharing of feelings. Try not to miss an opportunity anywhere in the exercises to talk honestly to your partner. We hope that you will be feeling more comfortable in making requests to your partner and in sharing feelings honestly. Attempt to express your thoughts in new and different words. Express your need for each other. Your body is now learning to give and receive tenderness and warmth: Let your words express these new feelings. Make your partner know how special a person he or she truly is.

You might also try out a different position. For instance, the female can lie on her stomach, with the male lying on his side, facing her and touching her entire body length, with his upper leg bent at the knee so that the leg rests across her legs. Slowly and gently caress her back from the neck to the waist. Talk to her while you are gently touching. Describe what you feel, how you feel, what you have noticed that is new to you. Ask your partner to tell you how it feels to be touched and caressed.

When you have finished the back caress, gently move your leg up and down her legs, feeling her skin with the inside of your thigh and with your calf, and exploring and touching with the instep of your foot. Tell her what you are doing, how it feels to you, and how you are feeling emotionally. Ask her to tell you how she feels, what she likes best, and how you can best please her. When you have finished, change places and accept her caresses. Make the caresses more gentle, tender, and mutual. Feel comfortable in simultaneously giving and receiving pleasure. During the first three exercises you have learned about your basic responses as well as your partner's. Now allow this to be a mutually enjoyable sensuous and sharing experience.

AFTERWORD

By this point, we hope that you and your partner are more aware and accepting of the natural responses of your body to non-genital touch and to the pleasures of sensuality. Couples often fall into a trap when the only touching they do leads to intercourse. Most of this touching is genital and oriented specifically toward sexual arousal. We hope that you have learned to appreciate new feelings of sensuousness and non-genital touch, that you now know what kinds of non-genital touch are most enjoyable to you, and what parts of your body are most responsive. Learning these facts about yourself, you have been able to share them with your partner and to communicate in a direct, comfortable way.

With a basic foundation of acceptance of touch and

your bodily reactions, with an emphasis on slowness, tenderness, warmth, sharing, and love, you can move on to become a more harmonious couple.

5   Genital Touching and Pleasuring

In doing the exercises involved with non-genital touching, you have probably become more comfortable with your natural bodily feelings as well as the reactions of your partner. Also, we hope that you have relearned the enjoyment of touch and sensuality without worrying about the pressure of goal-oriented sexual performance. Now that the base of slow, gentle, rhythmic touching has been established, you can build upon it by adding genital touch and using a more natural and integrated approach to whole body touch. The most important thing to keep in mind with these exercises is this: Now that you will be using genital touch, do not fall back into the trap of having all your interactions become genitally-oriented and aimed toward sexual intercourse. Rather, the genital touching should be preceded by non-genital touching, and the genital touching should be integrated with the non-genital. They should complement each other, rather than genital touch displacing the non-genital.

At this point, you will be continuing in the stage of exploring and learning to enjoy giving and receiving pleasure. The *goal* of sexual intercourse is not appropriate because it tends to raise performance anxiety. Instead, the emphasis in these exercises is a non-goal-oriented experience in integrating non-genital with genital touching and sensual feelings with sexual feelings. As with the non-genital touch, you should first focus on learning and accepting your feelings about your genital reactions and then teaching your partner about the type and location of touch that is most sensually and sexually enjoyable to you.

We suggest that you first read this chapter through alone, and then talk with your partner about it. Remember, the exercises are suggestions and guidelines set up to help you in the exploring and discovering process rather than rigid rules you must follow to prove your sexuality. You are doing this to be more aware of and accepting of your genital feelings and responses and to integrate these into your feelings as a sexual person. Then you will be able to convey this attitude to your partner in an open, honest exchange. You will also be better able to focus on and accept your partner's genital feelings and his or her sexual responsivity.

Each exercise is intended to take from forty-five to ninety minutes; however, this time assignment is flexible. You may want to separate some parts of the exercises and to do these totally independently of the program. Some couples will want to devote more time or time at a different point to doing the non-genital touch with clothes on, or to integrating the non-genital and genital touch. Remember to plan a relaxed time in which you surely will not be disturbed or feel hurried. Be sure to spend at least fifteen minutes on each exercise experience. Think of this as a further step toward learning about and accepting yourself as a healthy sensual and sexual human being.

First Set of Exercises For Chapter 5

Before beginning, sit and talk for about fifteen minutes about the highlights of your non-genital touching experiences, and discuss what you need to know about yourself to feel more comfortable with genital touch. Remind your partner what things you liked about the non-genital touch and describe how important it is to you to continue this pleasurable, tender interaction.

Hold hands as you go to take your shower or bath together. Soap and caress each other in the same enjoyable manner as before, with one addition: Wash your partner's entire body. As you reach the genital areas, name each part aloud such as penis, mons, scrotum, vagina, etc. This gives you practice in using sexual words. In giving verbal feedback, it is important that you feel comfortable in talking about genital areas. If arousal occurs during the bath or shower, simply accept it as a healthy and natural process; do not feel any pressure to do something about the arousal — simply accept it.

As you leave the bath, dry each other off including the genital areas in the natural progression of drying the body from top to bottom. Do not save the genitals for last. Include them as a natural part of your partner's body.

Then go to your bedroom and be sure that things are conducive to feeling comfortable and sensuous. Are you comfortable with the room lighting? Some people like it very bright, others like a more darkened room. However, be sure it is not so dark that you cannot see the details of your partner's nude body. If you like music to help you get into a more sensuous mood, then by all means put on some of your favorite music. Before beginning, spend some time just relaxing and making yourself comfortable.

Begin this phase of the exercises with the non-demand position you used in non-genital touch with the woman on her back and the man on his side, her feet or legs over his bent legs. The man will be the pleasurer for the first part of the exercise.

First focus on the relaxing and sensuous kinds of

non-genital touch that you have learned your partner appreciates the most. Also, kiss or orally stimulate particular non-genital body parts. Then with your right hand, begin to caress your partner's breasts very gently, as an extension of rubbing her chest and sides. When her partner begins doing this, the woman should close her eyes and, as pleasuree, be particularly aware of what rhythm and type of breast touch is particularly sensuous. Through the rest of this exercise, she should continue to keep her eyes closed and focus on the pleasurable sensation. She should not pressure herself into having to feel sexually aroused. Instead, she should simply accept her natural bodily sensual and sexual reactions. Remember, the role of the pleasuree is to be passive and to allow one to be receptive to and accepting of pleasure. The notion of being selfish and just taking in pleasure is difficult for some people to accept — especially so for those who always worried about pleasing their partners and ignoring their own needs and desires. Obviously, if you did that all the time, it would halt your relationship until you could really learn to enjoy your own sexuality. "Selfishness" is an important step in developing a healthy sexual relationship. Both the pleasurer and the pleasuree should think of the breasts as completely new parts of the body to discover and to explore. The pleasurer should view the breasts (and genital parts) in a very different and enjoyable way and feel comfortable in exploring a variety of touch experiences so that his partner might better understand her reactions.

Gradually focus more and more attention on breast stimulation. With the palm of the hand, start at the waist and move up to the neck with one long motion. Be careful not to press hard, because the breasts are usually quite sensitive, and you might inadvertently be causing your partner some discomfort. Trace the nipple with your fingertips, and see if it becomes more erect. This is usually a sign of arousal. Notice the different sensations in touch on an erect, as opposed to a non-erect, nipple. As you are caressing her breasts, be aware of and respond to any warm and tender feelings that you have.

Place your hand on your partner's opposite side so that you nearly surround her with your arm — your hand holding the arm, parallel with the breasts — so that in a slow continuous movement you draw your hand over the soft skin underneath the armpit, across both breasts to the other side, and then slowly back again. As you pass over a breast, if the nipple is soft, gently caress it until it is erect; if it is erect try a circular motion with the palm of your hand until it is soft.

Lifting yourself on your elbow for support, kiss and caress the breasts and chest area in general. Feel the different texture changes with your tongue.

At this point and throughout this exercise, the emphasis is on non-verbal communication, since talking can get in the way of bodily feelings. However, as pleasurer, you should be especially sensitive to any non-verbal signs of tension or anxiety in your partner. If you feel her tense up, back off a little in your particular activity, but do not remove yourself from body contact; that is, keep contact, but move back just a step or two. If kissing her breast makes her tense, and you feel it or she reports it, nonverbally move your kisses to her general chest area until she is comfortable again. Do not move away completely or interrupt the contact. Neither of you has made a mistake. It simply takes time and experience for each of you to relax and learn what is pleasurable in genital touch. Just stay with the feelings and the sense of learning and exploration. If you are anxious, remember that you are helping each other to get to know yourselves, and that your partner may be a little anxious too. Your relaxing will help to make your partner more comfortable and to feel more secure in the pleasuring. When the male has given his partner a variety of breast stimulation experiences, including touching the areola with just the palm of his hands, gently bringing the breasts as close together as they will go, and exploring the difference in separate versus simultaneous breast stimulation, the partners should change roles.

Since breast stimulation has already been done with the male during the non-genital touching, extensive exploration will probably not be necessary. However, you should at least explore the difference in feeling between an erect and non-erect nipple and how your partner enjoys having his nipples kissed. Some men find this very arousing while others don't. There are no right or wrong responses. You are engaged in a process of discovering how your body reacts to stimulation.

At this point, express your warmth by touching and kissing attractive parts of your partner's body. Be sure that these exercises end on a pleasant and warm note. Then sit and talk about both partner's feelings about breast touching — manually and orally. How does the woman feel about her breasts? Does the man enjoy looking at them and touching them?

Second Set of Exercises For Chapter 5

This exercise should be done with the pleasuree keeping the eyes closed and with a minimum of verbal interaction. Again, begin with a bath or shower. This time while soaping your partner's genital area, describe verbally and in detail such things as skin appearance, size, and attractiveness. Describe how you feel about touching the genitals and what you find particularly fascinating or nice about them.

The first time the woman should be pleasurer and the male pleasuree. He can lie on his back in a comfortable manner, eyes closed, relaxed, and passive. At this point he should concentrate on receiving pleasure and being receptive to learning which types of touch and stimulation he's most responsive to. She should assume a comfortable position, perhaps kneeling near his stomach, sitting, or lying beside him.

Before beginning the touching, visually explore his body, not focusing specifically on the genital region but allowing your eyes to range over the entire body. Then spend some time gently massaging and caressing your favorite non-genital body parts. As you do this, observe his genital region. Be aware of your feelings about an erect penis as opposed to a flaccid (non-erect) penis. A commonly-believed myth is that when the male has an erection, the woman must *do* something, such as have intercourse. An erection might indicate general excitement (often men feel this during, for example, a sports event or while wrestling with their children), good sensual feelings, or sexual arousal. Interestingly, even the male often believes the myth that an erection *must* mean sexual arousal, and he attempts intercourse even when he doesn't feel like it. Remember, you do not have to do anything with his erection except observe it and enjoy it without feeling any demand.

While massaging around the stomach area, simply lower your hand movement and touch his genitals. As you explore the genitals, name each part as you touch it — penis, glans, shaft, frenulum, scrotum, testes. As you touch, repeat the words until you feel comfortable with them. If at any time during the touching either of you feel any anxiety, do not remove your hand from your partner's body, but simply massage a body part with which you feel comfortable and allow yourself to relax. Take a few long, deep breaths, and if you are still anxious, hold your partner in your arms for a few minutes until the anxiety is gone. It is most important to stay close and comfortable. Each person must proceed at his or her own pace and comfort level.

As you explore the testes with your hands, notice which is larger and what the shapes remind you of. Remember that they are very sensitive. Be careful to move slowly and gently. Notice how the testes can be moved around inside the scrotum.

If your partner is circumcised, trace the head of the penis with your fingertips. If he is not circumcised, gently move the foreskin back and explore the head. If the penis is flaccid, gently and non-demandingly massage and caress it until it becomes erect. Keep your hand on the penis. Notice the pulse as blood collects in the penis and enjoy the feeling of its becoming erect. Place your hands in a cup-like curve and hold the scrotum. Notice how it changes as his penis becomes erect. If the penis is erect, either continue with non-genital touching or discontinue touching until the erection subsides. Note the differences in the penis and scrotum in the non-erect state.

The male should also be aware of his feelings as the erection subsides. Often males become anxious at this point, yet in reality it is nothing to be threatened about. An erection can decrease and then be regained if the male allows it to happen without his becoming anxious or making self-demands about being stimulated.

Run your fingers through his pubic hair. Notice the texture, thickness, and length. Place the heels of your hands below his genitals on the soft insides of his legs. Slowly, gently, and rhythmically move your hands up to his waist and back down again. Moving over the penis, repeat these motions several times.

Holding his penis in one hand, feel the softness behind the scrotum with the other. With a fingertip trace a line down to his anus. Then, flattening your hand, caress the inside of one leg while you continue to hold and gently squeeze his penis. Try to keep the rhythm of his breathing with the squeezing of his penis. Try gently pulling and squeezing at the same time. Move your other hand to his lower abdomen and move it in small circles.

Remember, the role of the pleasurer is to provide a variety of types of stimulation so that the pleasuree can discover the pattern of stimulation to which he can best respond. At this point you should be using only manual touch. (Oral stimulation of the genital area is dealt with in a different set of exercises.) When you feel reasonably comfortable with genital touch and you feel you have given your partner a pleasurable experience you can switch roles.

The woman can lie on her back and let herself relax and be comfortable. The male can also get himself in a comfortable position, whether sitting, kneeling or lying. It is important that he can see and touch his partner's body, including her genitals. Begin by touching your partner's favorite non-genital areas, and then let her guide your hands over her breasts. She should do the guiding with her hands over her partner's hands. The male should let his partner teach him what type of breast touch is most comfortable and stimulating to her. As much as possible, she should tell her partner what pleases her by touch and gesture rather than by speaking, but she should use verbal support or guidance if she feels the need for it.

In this kind of communication — primarily non-verbal — it is especially important to remember consideration for your partner. You want your partner to understand, so be considerate. Repeat your gestures or your words, and try to explain your feelings so your partner can be sure to understand and appreciate them.

At this point, the male might also enjoy kissing, sucking, or some other oral stimulation of either the areola or the entire breast. The female can guide him by moving his head, touching his forehead, or making some other mutually-understood gesture. The male should be careful as he sucks or kisses, because the breasts can be sensitive. Be aware of your partner's response and feeling.

Massage around the stomach, and then lower your hands and explore the genital area. Gently run your fingers through her pubic hair, and caress her stomach up to her waist. Be aware of the texture of the pubic hair and how it looks and feels. Place the heels of both hands below her genitals in the soft inner part of her legs. With both hands cupped over most of her pubic hair, move your hands rhythmically in small circles.

Spread the labia majora with your fingers. (see Figure 1, page 20). In exploring the genital area, your goal should be feel comfortable with the sight and feel of her genitals rather than to to worry about sexual arousal. Find the clitoris and the clitoral shaft, and look carefully at the labia minora. Notice how they surround the vaginal opening. Spread the vaginal opening with two fingers and notice the color and texture of the interior. Feel the warmth and dampness. Gently insert one finger into the vagina and notice how it feels. Touch the mons area, the perineum, and around the urethra. As you explore these areas, verbalize the names, and be aware of how comfortable you are using sexual words. Repeat the words until you feel comfortable with them.

Move slowly and gently, remembering that gentle touching and exploration is important. The clitoris can be especially sensitive, so rather than stimulating it directly you should run your fingers next to it on the clitoral shaft. As your partner becomes aroused, the clitoris becomes larger and withdraws under the clitoral hood. This is the body's way of protecting itself from discomfort. Direct clitoral stimulation can cause pain. Massage around the clitoral shaft, thereby indirectly massaging the clitoris.

The touching and exploring should be gentle and not aimed at sexual arousal. If your partner does become aroused, lubricated and responsive, remember to *respond* with her, rather than to feel the need to *do* something. Remember to use non-genital touching too, rather than focusing completely on the genital region. When you feel that you are more comfortable with genital touch, and you have provided your partner with a variety of stimulation techniques, you can stop the exercise.

To conclude, you might simply hold your partner in your arms, sharing your feelings of warmth and tenderness. Then you might want to get dressed and go downstairs and talk, or perhaps just lie in bed nude holding hands. Share your feelings — talk openly and frankly about them — about exploring your partner's genitals as well as how it felt for your genitals to be explored and caressed in a non-demanding way.

Third Set of Exercises For Chapter 5

During these exercises, both of you should have your eyes open so that eye contact can facilitate the communication. If you wish, use your favorite lotion to enhance the feelings of sensuousness, remembering either to warm it or to pour it on your hand first to warm before rubbing on your partner's skin. Also, you will be using hand movements to guide and teach your partner the places where certain types of touch make you feel particularly comfortable and responsive.

Couples often have a difficult time communicating about how they like having their clothes taken off. Often one partner undresses himself hastily and crudely undresses the other. Begin this exercise with both of you dressed, and let the woman undress the man first. She starts by looking at her partner fully clothed, and then mentally undresses him. Be sure both of you are relaxed; keep good eye contact, but keep the verbal interaction at a minimum so you can focus on the experience.

You might begin the undressing by playing in a teasing manner with the middle buttons on his shirt. Unbutton the shirt slowly, and while doing so put your other hand on his crotch and notice his reaction even with clothes on. After you have taken the shirt off, unbuckle his belt and pants, turn him around, and lower his outer pants half-way. Then slowly take off both shoes, and let him step out of his pants. Turn him around so he is facing you, look at him, and give him a big hug. Then slowly take off his underpants. Finally remove his socks and notice how you feel about your role in undressing him in a seductive and sensuous way. The male should be aware of his feelings as well during this part of the exercise. How does it feel to hug and kiss your partner — one clothed and one nude?

The male should then undress his partner. First do it visually. Then kiss her and hold her closely, and while doing so start in the middle of her back and run your finger up and down her zipper or buttons. Unzip or unbutton a little at a time and then stop and run your fingers around her back and arms. Take one shoulder of her blouse off at a time, stroking her arm at the same time. As you touch her back, check where the hooks on the bra are, and undo one strap at a time — don't take the bra off; just let it hang. Then turn her around and take her shoes off. Next take her skirt off, or roll her slacks down slowly and easily. Then turn her around so you face each other — notice how she looks with her panties on and bra hanging loose. As you slowly take off the bra and panties say the warm things you are feeling about your partner. When she is nude take her in your arms and get ready to begin the pleasuring.

In subsequent experiences in undressing your partner in sensuous and seductive ways you can vary these techniques according to your unique style — sometimes extremely seductively and sometimes very playfully. The important thing is to realize that undressing can be sensuous, seductive, and fun rather than just routine.

You can decide who will be pleasurer first. In deciding this, you might want to determine who has more discomfort *in giving*; let him or her be the pleasurer. In the pleasuring, the focus should be on attending to your partner's feelings and guidance carefully, and on involving yourselves in giving. Remember the give-to-get principle of mutual sexual satisfaction.

In the pleasuring you might want to try a different position. The pleasurer sits first on the bed, with back support from the wall or bedboard, or preferably from some soft pillows. This partner's legs should be spread far enough apart so that the other partner can sit between them.

The other partner — the pleasuree — needs back support too. Arrange some more pillows to allow support and to permit the pleasuree to be in a semi-reclining position. There is no set way to go about placing the pillows; just fix them so that both bodies are in comfortable and relaxed positions.

The pleasuree's legs will be over the pleasurer's. Be sure the pleasurer has full access to the entire body of the pleasuree.

As pleasurer, begin by caressing the genitals, perhaps using your favorite lotion. Go over the genitals as if your goal is to cover them completely with lotion. Do it slowly, tenderly, and rhythmically. Follow your partner's guidance. The pleasuree should feel free to move the hands to parts of the genitals that feel particularly sensuous and arousing.

Those who masturbate or have done some self-exploration and enhancement are in a particularly good position to understand their natural bodily reactions and to share these with their partner. Be open and honest with your partner. If you want him or her to explore a part of you that you're not sure of, help him or her do it. Do not be afraid to share your pleasure as you learn to respond as a healthy sensual and sexual being.

When you both are comfortable with your genital feelings, move on to touching non-genital body parts. Very often touching goes quickly from non-genital to focused genital touch. How does it feel to reverse that process? Allow the non-genital touch to be slow, tender, and rhythmic, and be very responsive to your partner's guidance and feelings. Try to make the non-genital as enjoyable as the genital touch, and as enhancing to your partner.

You can then switch roles of the pleasurer and pleasuree and repeat the same sequence. Afterwards, if you are comfortable doing so, lie in bed in the nude and share feelings about your experience — your awareness about giving and receiving non-genital and genital touching. You might want to share with your partner how you feel about initiating and how you feel about receiving. Be frank, direct, clear, and supportive in your verbal feedback to your partner. Probably the most important part to share is how you are feeling about your partner as a sensual and sexual person.

If you really cannot talk about your experiences, or if you cannot make yourself express your feelings of love and endearment as well as your feelings of pleasure or dislike about specific activities, you should consider the following remedies.

First, you can move back a step to an exercise you *can* talk about comfortably. There are no laws or rules telling what exercises must be done in what order. If necessary, then, go back to a comfortable spot and try that again. Second, you can discuss your problem of communication with your partner. If you have a good feeling you want to express but cannot, ask your partner about his or her good feelings. Make a common ground of discussion if possible. It may be that your partner can draw upon experience and concern for you and can help you express your feelings. Third, you can focus your attention on some activity and the feelings you have about it by approaching that activity directly. Ask your partner, very specifically, to try that activity, and if it is carried out, try to put into words your feelings as the activity proceeds. Finally, you might consider, together with your partner, asking for professional help in "unblocking" or freeing yourself for more comfortable and complete expression. In all these possibilities, however, you can and should focus your attention on *specific techniques* to increase sensuous responses. Do not make the mistake of asking general questions like "Do you really love me?"

Fourth Set of Exercises For Chapter 5

In this last set of exercises it is most important to integrate genital and non-genital touch, using eye contact and verbal exchange. Base the first half of the session on mutual touching, with a lot of spontaneity and sharing. Also, rather than be pleasurer and pleasuree, allow the exercise to be more unstructured, with simultaneous giving and receiving of pleasure.

After this, you can move to the so-called sex caress. To do this, return to the pleasurer-pleasuree approach, letting the male be the pleasurer first. The sex caress is an integration of genital and non-genital touching; it is both sensual and sexual. The key terms dealing with the sex caress are *slow, tender,* and *rhythmic*.

The pleasuree lies on her stomach; she can have her eyes open or closed, whichever feels more comfortable. Begin by massaging the back of the neck with both hands. Be sure the neck muscles are relaxed. Then gently move your hands down to about three inches above the tailbone and massage this area in smooth, rhythmic motions.

Next, move your hands to the backs of the thighs and then caress the buttocks. Bring your hands together at the small of the back, caressing this area, and, using the same motion, move back to the thighs. Do this several times and allow yourself to respond to feelings of sensuousness and sexuality.

Help your partner turn over. When you are both comfortable, gently place both hands on her thighs. With a smooth sweeping movement, move your hands up her thighs, over the genital area; bring them together at her stomach. Spread your hands in an outward movement toward both breasts. Bring her breasts together. Then caress back again with the same movement to the thighs. Be sure to touch the genital area fully, but do not concentrate on it. Rather, integrate the whole process. Do this several times, and attend to your own feelings of pleasure at your partner's enjoyment and responsiveness. By all means talk about your feelings. Continue the caressing movements until your partner asks you to stop them.

Then change roles and let the woman repeat the same series of exercises. However, she should use her own unique style.

There is one additional exercise which seems particularly effective. Typically a woman will not use her breasts actively; instead, she is passive while the male massages them. Active breast movement can be very enjoyable to the woman as well as to her partner. After hand-massage of the man's thighs, genitals, stomach, and chest, she can put some lotion on her breasts and repeat the same movements using her breasts rather than her hands. If you do this, notice the feelings in your breasts; often women find their breast responsiveness heightened by this experience. When you've done this long enough to decide whether it feels comfortable and arousing to you, have your partner lie comfortably on his side and put your hand on his chest with your front to his back and try to follow the rhythm of his breathing. Allow yourselves to breathe together. This can be a very warm, close, and intimate feeling. Share this with each other, and then allow yourselves to drift off to sleep.

AFTERWORD

This last exercise completes the basic core of the program to help you function more comfortably as a healthy sexual person and as a sensuous and sexual couple. You should feel comfortable with giving and receiving sensual and sexual stimulation in a relaxed, non-goal-oriented atmosphere. Your acceptance of both your own and your partner's sensual and sexual reactions and your acceptance of your own unique styles of giving and receiving pleasure are now more clear and positive. This kind of acceptance is a solid foundation for sexual functioning and communication.

6 Increasing Arousal and Sexual Response for Women

Until the research of Masters and Johnson, it was widely assumed that men were more interested and responsive to sexuality than women. Sex, in fact, was supposed by many to be the woman's duty. At best, according to this view, sex was tolerated because it allowed affection and physical intimacy, but the woman was not expected to look forward to, and actually to enjoy, sexuality and intercourse. At worst, sex was painful and degrading. The idea that the woman would enjoy sex more than the man was almost unheard of. However, Masters and Johnson found that, in fact, there are more similarities than differences in male and female sexual responsiveness. This conclusion suggests, among other things, that females and males have similar capacities for enjoyment.

Actually, women have the opportunity to enjoy sexual experience more than men, since they have the potential to have several orgasms in a row — to be *multiorgasmic*, as Masters and Johnson and other therapists say. On the other hand, the great majority of males can have only a single orgasm during each intercourse experience. Therefore, from the point of view of physiological response, the female could be thought of as more sexually-oriented than the male. At the very least, women should give themselves permission to express their healthy and normal sexuality. Full and enjoyable sexual activity and feeling are as much rights of the females as they are rights of the males.

NEW MYTHS REPLACE OLD MYTHS

In helping the woman better understand, accept, and enjoy her own sexuality, the goal is *not* to have a competition between partners. Rather, both should be aware of their own sexuality so that they might share that with their partner, and thereby enhance their sexual functioning as a couple. The major factor inhibiting this acceptance has been the massive misunderstanding regarding female sexuality. Unfortunately, recent findings about human sexuality have not been well presented in the media. They have resulted in the formation of new myths, such as the belief that the woman *must* have an orgasm at each sexual opportunity, or the belief that orgasm is the *only* measure of sexual satisfaction.

The most important concept to realize, and for both partners to accept, is that female sexual response is much more complex than male sexual response. It is not better or worse, more sexual or less sexual, but simply more complex.

VARIATIONS IN FEMALE RESPONSE

Typically, male sexual activity includes an orgasmic experience with each intercourse. Although there is some variability, and there is a difference in the psychological feelings of enjoyment and satisfaction, the orgasm itself is a relatively stereotyped response. Not so with female sexual response. The female may have no orgasms, one, or many. There is a good deal of variation in her psychological feelings of satisfaction. For example, there are times when the female will enjoy sex more if she has no orgasm, instead of one or many. Thus we conclude that orgasm by itself is a poor measure of sexual satisfaction in the woman.

This is not to say that orgasm is not important for the woman; it is an important part of her and a central component of her sexuality. However, it is not its only component. This must be accepted by the woman and her partner.

Sophisticated males may feel that they were bad lovers if their partner was not orgasmic at each sexual interaction. This is as harmful a sexual myth as the old myth that females were not supposed to enjoy sex. The reality is that orgasm is the natural culmination of effective sexual arousal. An orgasm cannot be willed or made to occur. The more the female (and her partner) work to bring about an orgasm, the less likely it is to occur. In the same way that male potency problems are often caused by performance anxiety, female non-orgasmic response can often be caused by focusing solely on trying to have an orgasm or demands and pressure from herself or her partner.

Learning to be sexually responsive and orgasmic is a skill which is gradually learned as the woman and the couple learn about, accept, and enhance her sexuality and their sexual functioning. Being sexually responsive and orgasmic are not mysterious processes that you must experience to be a real woman. We hope that, in self-exploration and non-genital and genital pleasuring, you have established a base of understanding and acceptance. These exercises will simply build on that base.

Very few females learn orgasmic response during intercourse. The great majority have their first orgasmic experiences through masturbation, foreplay, pleasuring, during cunnilingus (oral-genital sex) or during afterplay. Once you have learned to accept the feelings of orgasmic response, you can work with your partner in having orgasmic responses with him and in intercourse. It is most important to realize that orgasm is the same whether achieved through masturbation, foreplay, oral sex, or intercourse. There is no such thing as better or vaginal orgasms. Physically, all orgasms are the same. They are essentially a response to direct or indirect clitoral stimulation and are experienced as muscle contractions in the muscles around the vagina.

ACCEPTING THE FEMALE'S RESPONSES

The focus in these exercises is to increase sexual response and arousal and to make both partners more accepting of the female's responsiveness. The emphasis is not on having an orgasm, but rather on increasing arousal and responsivity. If the female becomes orgasmic, it is simply the natural culmination of the couple's working together in an increasingly sensual and sexual experience.

Orgasm is the natural result of sexual response. The key to multiorgasmic response is to continue stimulation and to encourage the female partner to let herself go. At the same time, she should give herself permission to continue. It will not help the female to become multiorgasmic if, when she first becomes orgasmic, she is distracted from enjoying her arousal. Neither will she become multiorgasmic if she makes that her goal and therefore pressures herself to perform. The woman should not try to be multiorgasmic, but should instead accept the state of orgasm as a pleasurable one and allow it to happen.

We would suggest that you read through the entire set of exercises separately, and then focus on one exercise at a time. Increasing arousal and sexual responsivity in these exercises is a function for the couple (not for the female to do alone or the male to do for the female).

First Set of Exercises For Chapter 6

This exercise is a very specific one to help the couple focus on increasing both trust and arousal. Because of the dating patterns in our culture, the female often learns not to trust the male and to be guarded and defensive. Also, she might have learned not to show or express arousal because the male would take advantage of her or use her. Such feelings serve to inhibit female sexual expression even in a very good relationship. Before beginning, talk about how your trust in each other has built up as a function of the sensuality and sexuality exercises. Note expecially how you have learned to give and to utilize supportive feedback. The female might share with her partner the importance of feeling supported and trusting; this makes it easier for her to feel sexually responsive and aroused.

You can start the exercise by bathing together. The male should be particularly indulgent of his partner's feelings of comfort. He should wash her gently, tenderly, and carefully. After the bath, he can take a big, fluffy towel and pat her dry.

To accentuate the feelings of trust even more, she may close her eyes and let him lead her sexually, taking care that she feels safe and cared-for; she can trust him. While her eyes are closed she can be aware of and build upon her feelings of trust that her partner is caring for her and watching out for her.

The position to be used during this exercise is a non-demand position. The male positions himself comfortably against a wall, bedboard, or perhaps cushions, with his legs spread. The female leans back on him with her back against his chest, and her legs within his. She might lean her head back on his shoulder. (See Figure 6) Before beginning the pleasuring, both should be comfortable. The male's hands should have easy access to her neck, breasts, stomach, vulva, and thighs.

Both partners can have their eyes closed and be aware of the feelings of warmth, intimacy and trust. The male should make his pleasuring movements slow, tender, and rhythmic. As he feels his partner's sense of trust increasing, he can gently guide her into opening her legs, and putting them on top of his. At this

Figure 6

point there will be almost total body contact and a feeling of greater sensuality and intimacy.

If her legs are open and spread, the vulval area is completely open and exposed. Women are taught not to sit that way, and in the sexual situation they often feel vulnerable. This time she can focus on her feelings of being cared for and trusting — where she can feel secure and able to express her sensuality and sexuality, rather than vulnerable and inhibited.

The male's pleasuring might intermix genital and non-genital touching, with a new emphasis on getting the rhythm of his touching in unison with the rhythm of her movement and responsivity. The emphasis in on consistent, arousing stimulation in the context of a non-demanding, trusting, and caring situation. Rather than focusing on one area or demanding sexual arousal, the touching pattern should be oriented toward developing the feelings of trust and caring. If your partner becomes aroused and sexually responsive, and if it appears that she might be orgasmic, simply continue with the same pattern and rhythm of sexual stimulation. A mistake that many males make is that when their partner becomes sexually aroused, they increase the speed or depth or pattern of stimulation to try to bring their partner to orgasm. Instead, what happens is that she may lose her arousal. She feels frustrated and demanded upon, while the male feels as though he's failed her and has failed as a lover. The usual key to female orgasmic response is consistent sexual stimulation which is given in a continued rhythm. The male simply goes with and follows his partner's movements and rhythm.

On the other hand, the woman might not be sexually responsive at all. She might simply be enjoying the sensuous, trusting, and caring feelings. She should feel comfortable, since the focus of this non-demand position is to allow her to build feelings of trust and comfort without a sexual demand or feelings of inhibition.

Allow the touching to continue in this position until both partners, but especially the female, are aware of and accepting the feelings of trust. You can end this exercise by breathing together. The male should be comfortably on his side, with the female putting her head against his upper back, with her breasts touching his back. She should try to get into the rhythm of his breathing. As you breathe together, be aware of the feelings of warmth, intimacy and trust. Verbally share these feelings, and perhaps you can allow yourself to drift off to sleep knowing that the major ingredients for female orgasm — sense of trust, affection, and an ability to be responsive and aroused without feeling inhibited — are now on solid footing. Feel free to repeat these or other exercises to increase the feelings of trust and comfort with uninhibited responsivity.

Second Set of Exercises For Chapter 6

Before beginning, sit and talk together about what you've learned about yourselves and each other in the non-genital touching and genital pleasuring exercises. Specifically, the female may want to discuss with her partner what she has learned so far about her response to sensual and sexual stimulation. She can discuss her desire to expand her feelings and reactions and share with her partner the orgasmic experience. She might also share with her partner the idea that it is easier for a woman than for a man to get turned off sexually. She might suggest what he can avoid doing to keep from turning her off in advertently. Also, if in the midst of a sexual interaction she does become turned off, the partners should discuss how they as a couple can handle it well rather than getting disappointed and angry with each other.

You can begin the exercise with a bath or shower. Make it relaxing, sharing, and a warm and mutual experience. The male should try to be especially aware of his partner's feelings and desires.

The male will be pleasurer and the female pleasuree. The female may keep her eyes open to facilitate interpersonal communication, or, if she would like, she can close them to be in better touch with her own feelings. Arrange yourselves in a position where the male leans back comfortably with his back supported by a pillow or cushion against either the headboard of the bed or the wall. The female should position her body comfortably between her partner's spread legs, lying on her back facing her partner, with her legs bent in a comfortable manner and resting on the mattress outside her partner's thigh region. This is the same position used in teaching ejaculatory control to the male. Of course, the position here of the female and male are reversed. Before continuing, be sure you are comfortable in this position. The male should have easy access to his partner's open vulval area as well as to her breasts. The female is able to touch her partner and to display affection and warmth if she wants to, but her major focus should be on accepting and building her own arousal and pleasure. (See Figure 7)

The male can begin his touching non-genitally, in a slow, tender, and rhythmic way to communicate to his partner his sense of love and caring. The genital touching can be gradually integrated into this but should not be overemphasized. As the male continues to touch, he should follow his partner's guidance. It can be by her hand over his, or her own movements, or verbal requests in terms of the rhythm of touching and caressing that she wants him to follow. By making clear requests the woman takes some responsibility for her own sexual pleasure and the enhancement of the couple's sexual functioning. The male might also use a light, teasing touch, moving from her neck to her vulval area, then up and around her abdomen and thighs in a natural, tender movement, next up to her breasts using the type of breast stimulation he's learned is most sensuous. The touch should be non-demanding, but allowing her to feel her sensuousness and to express her sexual arousal. At

Figure 7

this point, do not focus on vulval stimulation; rather, allow the touching to cover the entire body.

As she becomes more aroused and lubricated, gently put your two fingers in the vagina. Spread the vaginal lubrication throughout the vulval area, especially around the clitoral shaft. Then continue the rhythm of the non-genital and genital pleasuring to increase the level of sexual arousal. Be very aware of your partner's feedback. Rather than either partner demanding or forcing, simply accept and accentuate the sensual and sexual feelings.

Up to this point the genital touching should not include manual vaginal insertion. Many women have learned to react negatively to vaginal insertion; for some it is a turn-off, because there is often little vaginal feeling. Often the male initiates vaginal insertion and then focuses on and forgets about the other pleasuring techniques. Most women find that vaginal pleasuring is most sexually arousing when there is a concurrent focus on other bodily touch. What you as a couple will learn to do is increase vaginal feeling, and at the same time continue the pleasurable rhythm of body or clitoral touching.

With his index finger, the male explores the vagina to help his partner better identify and discriminate among areas of vaginal feeling and response. While doing the vaginal exploration with one hand, he should continue the comfortable non-genital touching. If at any time either partner feels pressure demands or discomfort, simply return to the non-genital and genital pleasuring. During this part of the exercise, the female may close her eyes so that she can focus more on her vaginal feelings. You can conceptualize the vagina as a "clock" with the section closest to the clitoris as "12 o'clock" and the part closest to the anus as "6 o'clock." The male should insert his index finger within the vagina, approximately two finger joints. Contrary to the popular myth (the deeper the insertion, the greater the feeling), insertion of two finger joints — about one and one-half inches — reaches the area of the vagina adjacent to the pubococcygeus muscle and the area of greatest vaginal feeling for most women.

The male should gently but firmly move his index finger around the vagina, saying something like, "This is 2 o'clock, 4 o'clock, etc.," "If this were my penis, how would it feel there?" This movement should be slow so the woman can identify the feelings. Also, the exercise can be interspersed with non-genital touching and, if you wish, temporarily removing the finger from the vagina. The female should give verbal and non-verbal feedback, identifying her feelings and guiding her partner in the vaginal touching. Sometimes, certain areas of the vagina will hurt. This is most often due to muscle separation in the vaginal wall. (Usually this condition is not very serious. It can be corrected by using exercises to increase vaginal feeling and responsivity. If the woman does experience pain, she might consider consulting a gynecologist.)

Other sections of the vagina might be especially sexually arousing. Many women find that at "4 o'clock" and "8 o'clock" with two finger joints' insertion, the sexual feelings are most pleasurable. This is where the nerve bundles of the pubococcygeus muscle are most prominent. During the exercise, the male should move slowly, and allow his partner to be aware of her intravaginal feelings. This might be the first time that she, and you as a couple, have ever had this experience, so do it slowly and gently so the feelings can better be felt and discriminated. Women who are unable to discriminate intravaginal feelings will need more time doing the vaginal responsivity exercises.

You might do the intravaginal finger exploration only once or as many as ten times. The female should tell her partner to stop either when she feels he can understand her vaginal feelings or when she has learned enough from that experience. Feel free to do this part of the exercise on several different occasions in order that both partners feel more comfortable with intravaginal contact and both learn about vaginal feeling and responsivity.

Throughout this exercise, both of you should be focusing on the warm and tender feelings which, more than any specific sex technique, facilitate arousal and sexual response. After the intravaginal exploration, continue to do non-genital touching, staying together and enjoying the pleasuring.

If you are working on a program to improve the male's sexual functioning, you can then go on to that. Or the female can then do the type of pleasuring with her partner that he particularly enjoys. While she is doing this pleasuring, she should especially enjoy the experience of returning the caressing and enjoyment that her partner gave her.

Afterwards, talk about what you learned about female arousal and intravaginal exploration and sensitivity. Both should feel free to talk about what additional things they need to learn about female arousal, and, even more importantly, what each can do to feel more comfortable with the expression of normal, healthy female sexual responsivity.

Third Set of Exercises For Chapter 6

This exercise includes the use of an oil or lotion to make you feel more sensuous. The lotion also has the advantage of providing a somewhat desensitizing effect for vaginal secretion. Choose a lotion that you both enjoy. The pleasuring should begin utilizing the female non-demand position used in the first set of exercises. Both partners can have their eyes open, and the female might hold and caress her partner while he is doing the pleasuring.

The male can continue to integrate the non-genital and genital touching he has used previously, as well as intermixing this with the things he has learned about his partner from the previous two non-demand positions. Particularly important is that the female guide her partner in the type of intravaginal manual stimulation she finds most enjoyable and arousing. The male should continue the pleasuring until he is aware that his partner is allowing her feelings of sensuality and sexuality to be more expressive — in other words, that she feels comfortable in expressing herself in this non-demand position. When the male feels this is happening, he should check it out with his partner to see if she feels comfortable in being sexual in this non-demand position. The checking out and feedback can be verbal (saying "Do you feel into it?" or "Do you feel yourself sexy?") or non-verbal (touching her navel, using your hand to close her eyes) or any signal you mutually agree on. If the female signals no, simply stop the exercise and go back to it later; or, continue and then allow the exercise to end and talk about what feelings you want to develop to make the female feel more comfortable, trusting, and responsive.

If the signal is positive, the female should remain where she is and the male should get up on his knees and kneel over his partner from a side position. The male can then examine his partner and help her move into a more comfortable position; i.e., stretch her legs out, put a pillow under her head, or put her arm in a more comfortable position. From this position the male should orally stimulate (by kissing, licking, orally caressing) her body from the top of her head to her mons. At the same time, his hand can be manually stimulating the lower part of her body from her mons to the bottoms of her feet. (See Figure 8) The stimulation should begin by being light and teasing, and in a natural, rhythmic, and most important, *slow* flow, become more focused and directed. Eventually, the male can orally stimulate her breasts using a kissing, licking, and then sucking movement while simultaneously manually stimulating the labia, clitoral shaft, and then into the vagina where there is most vaginal feeling. It is important that the stimulation be

Figure 8

consistent and in rhythm with the female's movement and feeling. The female should feel free to direct her partner's touching and the rhythm. Remember, it is *her* arousal and response, and only she knows what feels most sensual and sexual.

Contrary to all the myths, no one knows more about female response and sexuality than the woman herself. Neither partner should push or try to force response or orgasm. Remember that both are natural results of accepting, guiding, and staying with sensual and sexual feelings. The woman should give herself permission to let go and abandon herself to feelings of pleasure and sexual responsivity, allowing herself to feel "sexually selfish" during this experience.

End this exercise by going with and staying with the positive sexual feelings. Lie in bed and talk about your feelings about the female's sexual responsivity. Then, if you desire, you might talk about the male's sexual responsivity or go on to mutual pleasuring or on to intercourse.

Fourth Set of Exercises For Chapter 6

Before beginning this set of exercises, you might want to sit together over a drink or cup of coffee and discuss the changes you've experienced and your feelings about female sexuality and responsivity. Check each other out. Does the male feel comfortable with his partner's arousal, or is he threatened by it? Is the female trusting and accepting of her sexual feelings, or does she feel vulnerable or inhibited? Is orgasm still seen as something of overwhelming importance of is it a part of you as a couple and a natural consequence of the female's sexual responsivity? Is responsivity, arousal, and orgasm a natural, flowing response of the couple, or is it still the female's problem for which the male puts pressure on himself and her to bring it about?

If you feel comfortable with the experiences of the

non-demand positions, feel free to talk more and focus more of your time on the non-demand techniques and feelings.

This exercise begins with mutual pleasuring, using both non-genital and genital techniques, and manual and oral stimulation. The couple should feel together as a couple, allowing their feelings of sexual responsivity and arousal to build together. The rhythm is that which will usually be utilized in foreplay. Sometimes the female is the initiator and pleasurer, sometimes the male, but most often there will be a comfortable interchange of giving and receiving pleasure and utilizing slow, tender, and rhythmic touching to increase each other's feelings of responsivity. Remember, it can be sexually very exciting to be aware of and enjoy the responsivity of your partner.

When both partners are feeling aroused, the couple should use the female superior intercourse position. (See Figure 9) Rather than moving immediately toward intromission, explore the feelings in this position. It is a good position for verbal and non-verbal communication and it gives the female greater range of movement that other positions give. The male should feel free to caress his partner's breasts as well as touching and caressing her thighs, while she can take his penis and rub it around her thighs, clitoral shaft, and vaginal opening. In doing this, continue to work together as a couple, enjoying both receiving and giving pleasure. The female will determine when to initiate intromission. She can do this when she is well lubricated and feeling sexually aroused and comfortable.

Intromission is easily accomplished by sliding back on the penis on a forty-five degree angle. Once intromission is accomplished, you will be doing the "quiet vagina" exercise. This simply means the female will allow the penis to touch the most sensitive parts of her vagina and will just enjoy the sensations of the penis in the vagina without major thrusting movements. There will be a need for some minimal movement in order to maintain the erection; the female can initiate this by slow non-demanding thrusting. She should be especially aware of the positive feelings in her vagina and thoughout her whole body. She might want to experiment with contracting the pubococcygeal muscles while she is doing the coital thrusting. She may be orgasmic during this time; however, the goal is not to be orgasmic, but rather to be fully accepting of her sexuality and expecially the positive feelings of the penis in her vagina. The quiet vagina can also be very enjoyable for the male. You can continue the quiet vagina for at least twenty minutes, and longer if you wish. During the time, touch each other, be aware of and responsive to other sensual and sexual feelings, and bring together and integrate all the feelings of the non-demand positions but especially the feelings of security and being cared about.

The male may also stimulate the clitoral area manually while his penis is in the vagina. Many couples find that this simultaneous clitoral and vaginal stimulation greatly adds to the woman's sexual responsiveness.

You can end this exercise by proceeding to active intercourse. However, rather than doing so quickly, slowly increase the amount of movement. Allow the woman to initiate and guide the rhythm of the movement.

Afterward, discuss the feelings of the quiet vagina. The woman might start by reporting what she found to be the most positive thing about her intravaginal sensitivity — whether she experienced any differences in her reaction to his penis, or whether she enjoyed the minimal movement more than more active movement. The male might share his feelings about the experience, how it felt to be less active in intercourse, how the vagina felt to his penis, and whether he would like to use the quiet vagina again in the future. The male can reassure his partner that her being sexually active and assertive is not a sexual threat or turn-off for him. Decide how you as a couple want to continue to work together to develop responsivity and orgasmic response.

AFTERWORD

At this point you as a woman and you as a couple should be comfortable with female sexuality and responsivity. Awareness of and enjoyment of responsivity will continue to build and grow as you integrate the exercise experiences into your entire lives and sexuality. It is important that both partners understand and accept the complexity of female sexual response. Remember, mutual satisfaction is a much better criterion of sexual satisfaction than is orgasm.

Figure 9

7 Increasing Vaginal Feeling and Response

One of the major myths which has had a negative influence on female sexuality is that there are two types of orgasms — clitoral and vaginal. The myth states that only a vaginal orgasm is truly a mature, pleasurable orgasm. In fact there is only one kind of female orgasm. Female orgasm is mainly a result of clitoral stimulation — either brought about by manual or oral stimulation of the clitoral area during pleasuring and foreplay or afterplay or by indirect stimulation of the clitoral hood during intercourse. The feelings of the orgasm are experiences in the muscles generally around the vagina and specifically around the clitoris. Whether an orgasm is obtained through masturbation, foreplay, oral sex, intercourse, or afterplay, the same orgasmic response is brought about by direct or indirect clitoral stimulation. Therefore, from a physiological point of view, there is no difference between orgasms obtained during intercourse and orgasms attained by any other method of sexual stimulation. As Masters and Johnson found, an orgasm is an orgasm. There is no such thing as mature vs. immature orgasms or vaginal vs. clitoral orgasms.

With this myth put aside, many women do feel that they would like to have more awareness and feeling in their vaginas, and to be able to experience orgasm during intercourse. This is a perfectly good and acceptable goal as long as each woman and her partner realize that their sexual functioning is not a failure or a disappointment if orgasm is not obtained during intercourse. In fact, many women use concurrent clitoral stimulation (either by partner or by self) to heighten the probability of being orgasmic during intercourse.

The set of exercises below is designed to be used by the woman independently of her partner to increase vaginal feeling and responsivity. Read the entire series of exercises through, and then do them one at a time. It is your choice as to whether you want your partner to read them also and discuss them with you, or whether you would like this to be your own project.

FAMILIARITY AND ENHANCEMENT

Enhancement of the woman's response to sexual stimulation is necessarily aided by her awareness of her own body and her feelings of sensuality and sexuality.

Familiarity with your anatomy will aid you in providing for yourself a program of exercise and awareness. By now, you have probably increased your awareness of your body and increased acceptance of your sensuality and sexuality from the exercises on self-exploration and enhancement, non-genital pleasuring, and genital pleasuring. This set of exercises will make you aware of and sensitive to a specific part of your body — your vagina.

Variation in size, shape, color, and texture is to be expected in all areas of the body. Muscle tone also will differ from one person to another, as well as from one area of the body to another. Although the vagina does not have the number of sensitive

nerve endings found in the clitoris, there are nerve endings —
especially in the exterior one-third of the vagina. Muscle tone within
the vagina has an even more important influence over the amount
and quality of vaginal feeling and responsivity. Not only does the
muscle tone influence vaginal feeling for the woman, but it also
influences the amount of sexual pleasure felt by the male during
intercourse. If the vagina is open and gaping, there is minimal
friction or feeling as the penis moves inside the vagina and thus the
female will feel little or no pressure of movement. Likewise, the
male will feel little contact. The exercises below will help to improve
muscle tone. Thus, the exercises are valuable for practically all
women. If muscle tone is very poor, the improvement can be great;
improvement can be from good to even better in women whose
muscle tone is reasonably good.

PAINFUL INTERCOURSE

Sometimes women complain of painful intercourse. There can be
many causes of this, but often a primary cause is weakness or tears
in the vaginal walls. The muscle tone exercises can result in stronger
and better tone by strengthening the muscles around the vaginal
walls, thus eliminating pain during intercourse. If there is continued
pain or there are other problems, of course, do not hesitate to consult
your gynecologist.

The vagina is a very flexible and adaptable organ.
It can easily adjust to penises of varying sizes. A common myth is
that size of penis influences vaginal feeling and responsivity. There
is also the myth that some penises are too small to be felt and that
some are so large as to be painful. In reality, the vagina can adapt to
penises of all sizes. Penis size has nothing to do with sexual
responsivity.

The muscle that most affects vaginal feeling is the
pubococcygeal muscle (referred to as "PC" below) which is the

master sphincter of the pelvis. This muscle presents nerve bundles in the vagina at various positions, depending on the tone and the location of the muscle. Doing PC and other vaginal exercises tones up the vaginal muscles and makes the vaginal walls firmer. By tightening and exercising the PC, the woman can pull the walls of the vagina together, moving the nerve bundles into their most sensitive position to be stimulated and responsive during intercourse. This occurs when the PC is directly in contact with the penis; the nerves are highly responsive during penile thrusting.

By doing vaginal exercises, women can to learn to identify and to intensify vaginal feelings and responsivity. These exercises, in conjunction with the exercises on self-exploration and enhancement, exercises on increasing arousal and responsivity, and exercises on increasing enjoyment of intercourse, will help you learn about and enjoy vaginal feelings.

It is important to be aware that vaginal muscles are like any other muscles in one's body. In order for the exercises to be effective, they must be done regularly and consistently. All exercises should be done at various intervals throughout the day so the muscles will not become fatigued or tender. If soreness develops, temporarily cut down on the number and then gradually work up to the prescribed number. At first, you will find little noticeable change, but as you continue with the exercises you will find that vaginal feeling will increase gradually. You will have no proof of your consistency and intent for a week or so, and the reward will be small at first. However, the long-term rewards will be great enough to increase your dedication to the improvement of both your body and your sex life.

First Set of Exercises For Chapter 7

The first thing you must do is to identify the PC. The easiest way to locate the PC muscle is to stop your flow while urinating. The muscle you use to stop the flow is the PC muscle. If you have a difficult time stopping the flow, this would suggest that the PC is weak. If you have a difficult time identifying the muscle, simply sit on the toilet with your legs far apart and lift your body a little off the toilet seat. This should facilitate your stopping the flow. Start and stop the flow several times to identify this muscle correctly.

Once you have identified the PC muscle, you can then begin to exercise it to tone the vaginal sensations. The first exercise is to tighten the PC muscle, hold for three seconds, and then release. Repeat this exercise ten times in succession — it will take you only about a minute. During the first week, do this three times *each* day; that is, complete ten repetitions three times daily. After that, do another PC muscle exercise — rapidly tense and relax it.

This very simple exercise closely approximates what the major sphincter muscle does involuntarily at orgasm. Tense and relax the PC muscle rapidly ten times; do this three times a day, right after you complete the first exercise (tightening and holding the PC muscle). Altogether, these steps in this part of the program will take you less than five minutes to complete.

As with any muscle-toning program, consistency is of the utmost importance. Make sure that you set up a schedule for yourself so that you can monitor yourself and be sure the exercises are done every day in a regular fashion. Some women keep a little 3 x 5 card with them, and note each time they do the exercises. Others keep a chart on the bathroom mirror, on the refrigerator, or under their pillow. The important thing is to set up a monitoring program which will help you be consistent in your exercising.

The exercise can be done anytime and anywhere, and others will not even be aware you are exercising the PC muscle. For instance, you can do it while driving your car, while at work, or while waiting your turn to bowl or tee up.

Remember that it will probably take a few weeks

before any large difference will be noticeable; the effects will be gradual, but eventually very worthwhile for you and your partner.

After one week, increase the exercise to twenty repetitions three times a day. Then one week later, increase the exercise to thirty repetitions three times a day. Continue the thirty repetitions for a week or two. By this time you should be feeling a noticeable difference and in fact you should be able to see and feel the movement of the vaginal floor. You can observe this, if you wish, by lying on your back and using a hand mirror to see the actual movement of the vaginal floor as you contract the PC. Notice the difference in vaginal sensations, and notice the heightened vaginal awareness and feelings.

Second Set of Exercises For Chapter 7

Once you are used to the first exercise — whether it be two days later or a few weeks later — continue with that and add a second exercise. The time to do this exercise is when you are sitting or lying down and feeling relaxed. Concentrate for a few minutes on deep, rhythmic breathing. Then, each time you inhale, raise and tighten all your pelvic muscles in a lifting effort so that the entire muscle structure of the pelvis is tightened as you lift. Then relax the pelvic muscles completely as you exhale. Try to do this at least ten times. It will take you only a minute or two. Begin these ten repetitions three times a day. Set up some easy monitoring system for yourself to be sure you get in three sessions daily. In addition to strengthening pelvic muscles, these exercises allow you some time each day to relax.

Consistent and regular exercise of the pelvic muscles should show you a distinct difference in movement of your body as you continue to tense and relax. After three or four weeks, you will observe a difference by putting your hand on your pelvis and noting the increased muscles.

Third Set of Exercises For Chapter 7

Once you have integrated the first two exercises into your regular routine, you can begin this third one, which calls on a slightly different pattern of muscles. When you have finished the second muscle exercise (raising and tightening the pelvic muscles at inhale and relaxing at exhale), simply relax and breathe regularly for a minute or so. Then relax while inhaling, but now, as you exhale, press down with all the muscles in your lower abdomen, as if you were trying to expel something from both the vagina and the bowel. Relax while inhaling, and press while exhaling. Do this exercise ten times, and try to do it three times a day. It would be best to do this right after you have done the second exercise. Together, both exercises (ten repetitions of each) will take you between five and ten minutes. It is worthwhile both in terms of developing your vaginal and pelvic feelings, as well as a relaxing interlude to yourself during the day.

In addition to their uses in the sensuality and sexuality program, these three exercises are also utilized in preparing for natural childbirth. The third exercise has also been found useful in helping women to relieve pain during menstruation and to facilitate bowel movements, since it strengthens the muscles needed for these functions.

AFTERWORD

The purpose of these exercises is for you to build up the muscle tone in the vagina and pelvis. By being more aware of the feelings in these areas, you can better integrate them into your feelings about yourself as a sensual and sexual person. You will be doing these exercises on your own, but if you wish, you can utilize your partner to help you either in the monitoring of the exercises or in giving you feedback about the differences in vaginal tightness and movement.

Women are not taught to be aware of and enjoy

vaginal and pelvic feelings. In doing these exercises you have learned to feel positive about these areas of your body, and at this point the tone of the vaginal and pelvic muscles should be much improved. The major way that you will be utilizing this improvement is during foreplay and intercourse. Subsequent exercises on increasing arousal and responsivity will help you and your partner integrate these exercises into your pleasuring styles. The difference in vaginal and pelvic tone and feeling will allow intercourse to be a more satisfying experience.

A final point deserves mention. As with any type of exercise or muscle-tone program, it is important to follow through with continued practice. The foregoing exercises were designed to improve muscle tone and vaginal responsivity, and in order to sustain these improvements, it is suggested that you continue these exercises as part of your daily living. Otherwise, the muscles will gradually lose tone and vaginal responsivity will decrease over time. Therefore, we suggest that you follow up with a maintenance program by exercising once a week. In this way you will continue to maintain good vaginal tone and responsivity.

Increasing Arousal and Potency for Men

Sometime in their lives, approximately 95% of males have a potency problem: either the inability to obtain erection or the inability to keep an adequate erection to enable the male to engage in intercourse. Males can be notorious braggarts about sexual prowess, and they often deny sexual doubts or difficulties. In reality, many males suffer discomfort or disenchantment from the myth-based cultural expectation that the real man is able and willing to have sex with any woman, any time, in any situation. Such an expectation puts a tremendous amount of performance stress on the male.

Very seldom is there any physical or medical reason for potency problems. They almost always relate to psychological factors in the individual or couple. However, each specific individual's potency problem should be checked out with a urologist. The major cause of potency problems is performance anxiety. The male is so concerned with proving himself or performing up to expectations that he becomes anxious, and that anxiety interferes with his sexual responsivity and potency. When a male feels tense or anxious, these feelings are physiologically incompatible with feelings of sensuality and sexuality. In other words, when an individual feels performance anxiety, worry, tension, or pressure, his sexual responsiveness and his positive emotions can easily be inhibited.

The second major psychological cause of potency problems is a negative emotional reaction, such as guilt, hostility, uncertainty or ambivalence. If either partner feels guilty or ambivalent about his or her sexual involvement, the guilt will interfere with sexual responsivity and arousal.

In order to increase responsivity and arousal, no matter what the interfering problem, the couple must work together in a cooperative, sharing manner. Lack of responsivity and potency should not be assumed as the problem of the male alone, but rather as a problem of the couple together. Increasing responsivity and making each other comfortable with potency is the couple's task. In learning to help the male increase his responsivity and be comfortable with his potency, the female can also learn to accept and enjoy her own sexuality. The first step for the couple is to discuss their desire to work together to increase feelings of arousal and potency.

CONCENTRATION AND FAILURE

The most important point to remember is that one cannot *will* an erection (produce an erection by making self-demands). If a man has had difficulty in either getting or maintaining an erection, he may tend to concentrate on his penis and attempt to bring about an erection. Usually this is self-defeating. The more he concentrates on, and works at, achieving erection, the less success he will have. An erection is a naturally evolving consequence of effective sexual stimulation and feeling; it is not something to be striven for and achieved. When the male focuses all his attention on his penis, he takes himself out of the sexual situation and plays a spectator role. Rather than being focused on the sexual situation, the partner, and the enjoyment of the touching and pleasuring, the spectator focuses on himself and the state of his penis. Instead of being actively involved in the sexual situation — which naturally results in an erection — he is passively observing his state of sexual arousal and his penis. This does not result in sexual arousal.

CONCENTRATING ON INVOLVEMENT

A highly useful way to increase sexual arousal and make the couple (not only the male) comfortable with potency is for the couple to be actively involved in sensual and sexual stimulation. Rather than focusing on or worrying about any potency problem, the couple should focus on giving pleasure to each other and being aware of each other's pleasurable feelings. In this way the couple breaks the vicious cycle of worrying about sexual performance and concentrates on the enjoyment and responsivity which allows them to become sexually aroused. In allowing his natural responsivity to develop, the male will cultivate more positive sex feelings and stimulation.

In this sex awareness and enhancement program, the emphasis is on the male and female working together to develop a positive, sexually-enhancing relationship. For arousal and potency problems, positive feelings and effective sexual stimulation can be constructively used to counteract past fears, anxieties, and worries about sexual performance.

You have learned that you can share with each other in a non-demanding, non-goal-oriented manner. You can employ this same approach to teach yourself and your partner ways to increase responsivity and to feel much more comfortable with potency.

An erection is a psychophysiological response which is the natural reaction to effective sexual stimulation and the acceptance of these feelings. Sexual arousal leading to erection is the natural outcome of positive emotions and the male's being in touch with his sensual and sexual feelings as well as those of his partner.

We suggest that you read this set of exercises over separately, and then discuss it fully. It is especially important to beware of the traps of potency problems so that you can avoid them.

First Set of Exercises For Chapter 8

Begin the exercises by sitting together, holding hands gently and tenderly, and discussing how you felt and what you learned in the non-genital and genital pleasuring exercises. Discuss any personal and sexual traps that you have experienced and how you will avoid falling into them. Resolve to work together in an enjoyable, non-demanding way to learn to give and receive sexually arousing stimulation.

Begin the exercises with a relaxing and sensuous shower. Wash each other off, including the genitals, and then rub and pat your partner dry. Get yourselves into a comfortable pleasuring position, and let the female assume the role of pleasurer and the male that of pleasuree. She might begin with non-genital touching, then proceed to genital touching, and then back to non-genital. The male should simply accept the feelings of pleasure and allow natural responsiveness to occur. In a non-demanding way, she continues the pleasuring until a firm erection occurs. At that point, the touching and pleasuring can be replaced with simply lying closer together until the erection subsides. Both partners should be aware of their feelings as the erection subsides. Is there a feeling of anger? Fright? Anxiety? Worry? Tension? Relief? When the penis has returned to the flaccid state, the female may resume non-genital pleasuring, then genital touching, and then using her own unique combination of touching.

Instead of concentrating on achieving an erection, the male can simply relax, and enjoy and accept the pleasuring. When an erection naturally occurs, again cease activity until it is lost completely. If an erection does not occur, that is all right too — simply proceed with the pleasuring. The focus is not on getting an erection but on accepting and enjoying sexual stimulation. The male should just let himself go and allow his sensual and sexual feelings to build and allow himself to enjoy.

Then the male assumes the role of pleasurer and focuses on his partner's enjoyment. He does not have to worry about himself or his responsivity. He is free, however, to be aware of his feelings of giving pleasure and seeing his partner respond. Often an erection will occur naturally. If so, the male should let it subside.

Do this exercise enough times so that both partners are comfortable with his achieving and losing erection without feeling anxiety or pressure. It is important to realize that for the average couple the male's erection becomes hard and then somewhat flaccid usually from one to three times during a typical thirty minute foreplay period. A couple having problems with potency will push the male to erection and become anxious or panicky if the erection subsides. This worry or anxiety reaction is what causes the penis to become flaccid, and then the worry and pressure to regain the erection inhibit the responsivity to the point of blocking the penis from becoming erect.

If the male finds that he is troubled by recurrent worries about getting or losing an erection, he might focus on a sexual fantasy such as making love to his ideal woman, or being caressed by hands, or having intercourse swinging from a bell tower, or any fantasy he can enjoy.

The couple can easily learn to be comfortable with the erection becoming softer. They might want to repeat this exercise more than once until the comfort level is high and the anxiety and pressure to perform is low. Each exercise should end with the couple switching roles, and the male giving his partner the type of pleasuring experience he has learned she is most responsive to. Do this unless you have decided to use the exercises to increase female responsivity, and if so proceed with those. (See Chapter 6.)

After the exercise, lie in bed nude and give each other feedback about the feelings you had as the erection became flaccid, as the erection was regained, and about the manner of stimulation you enjoy giving and to which you are responsive. Notice the difference: You are working together comfortably rather than making demands and functioning under pressure. Also, notice the decrease in anxiety and worry as you both learn to accept the naturally-occurring responsivity and erection.

Second Set of Exercises For Chapter 8

During this set of exercises, you will be using the female-superior intercourse position. (See Figure 10) You will not actually be engaging in intercourse, but it is important that you be able to reduce anxiety and pressure and to increase responsivity and comfort with potency when the penis is near the vagina. The couple should be comfortable and at ease in this position, perhaps with a pillow under the male's head. The female should have easy access to the male's genitals, and her legs — expecially her thighs — should be supported with a pillow. The male should take the role of pleasuree and simply accept and enjoy the pleasuring and touching, although he can also hold and caress his partner. The male can feel free to guide his partner and make specific requests for her to do the kind of pleasuring which causes him the most arousal.

The female should begin by massaging her partner's arms and chest, then running her fingers over his face, highlighting his features, and finally massaging his genital area, beginning at the

Figure 10

inner thighs, working up and over the penis and pubic hair, over the stomach and then back again in the same movement. When her partner gets an erection as a natural outcome of feeling pleasure and accepting his responsivity, she simply ceases activity until the erection becomes soft. She should simply accept the penis in this state — a natural result of stopping touching and pleasuring; neither partner should feel worried or panicky. The female should then return to her own unique style of non-genital and genital pleasuring, and as the receptivity and responsivity increase, an erection will naturally occur.

The female can then take the penis in her hand, gently caressing it and rubbing it around her vulval area. Begin rubbing it around the mons, then move to the clitoral shaft, down to the labia, and finally around (but not into) the vaginal opening.

If at any point you notice your partner becoming tense or anxious or the erection becoming softer, still continue movement and manipulate or fondle the penis, and move back a step or two until both of you are again feeling comfortable and responsive; move forward after you both feel relaxed and receptive. Repeat this sequence of the male achieving erection with the penis around the vulval area, allowing it to become soft, and finally being restimulated once more to erection.

You might do this exercise just twice or you might want to do it several times over a period of days until both partners feel comfortable with the penis's periodic flaccidity as a natural consequence of the cessation of sexual stimulation and feeling. Remember, in a typical foreplay situation the erection will not always remain "hard"; rather, it is common to have the erection become soft two or three times. This is normal and should be accepted as such.

End the exercise either with the female being the pleasuree or using mutual stimulation where you feel warm and close, and enjoy being together. It is important that the female feel involved with the exercises, and that she feel the appreciation and caring in her partner's gestures and verbal responses.

Third Set of Exercises For Chapter 8

You will be using a combination of the male non-demand position and the female superior intercourse position. The couple begins the exercise with the female non-demandingly pleasuring her partner with a variety of non-genital, oral, and manual genital techniques. As soon as the male achieves erection, she then stops the stimulation, but this time the male should concentrate on trying to maintain the erection. Almost invariably the erection will be lost. This should vividly illustrate to the couple that when they concentrate on an erection and try to maintain it, it is lost instead, and the penis becomes flaccid. The only way to maintain an erection is to focus on your immediate sexual situation, accept the sensual and sexual stimulation and allow yourself to be responsive. Do not focus on the penis. This exercise is intended to demonstrate clearly the negative effects of trying to focus on an erection; one demonstration should be enough. Unlike all of the other technique-exercises in this book, this is a negative one; it should not be repeated.

After the erection is once more regained by the female's stimulation of the penis against her vulval area, again allow the penis to become flaccid. Next, rather than letting the female restimulate the male with his merely accepting it, focus on his trying to get an erection. That is, the male should try to help along his erection, working to achieve it. At this point, he probably will not have an erection.

The male should notice the pressure and tension he puts himself under, and how less sensual and enjoyable the feelings are when he tries to will an erection. Also, he can notice that rather than being part of and enjoying the pleasuring, he has become a spectator of his penis arousal. Be being a spectator, he shuts off the enjoyment and arousal of actively being involved by the sexually arousing situation.

The female should notice how it has become demanding, goal-oriented work to keep the erection rather than enjoyable pleasuring. She should also notice how frustrated and worried she has become, and how out of touch she is with her partner as he works *alone*.

The couple should be aware of the concentration traps so they can help each other avoid them in the future. While relaxing in bed nude, the couple might want to share their feelings about the differences between being together in a non-demanding atmosphere, mutually pleasuring one another and accepting the naturally occurring responsivity and erection as opposed to working alone, worrying, feeling tense, being a spectator, trying to will an erection, and being goal-oriented.

The couple should then move to the female-superior intercourse position, and the female should use a variety of pleasuring techniques with an emphasis on flirtatiously teasing her partner in a non-demanding manner. After the full erection occurs. she then rubs the penis around her clitoris and labia, against her thigh, and around her vagina. Both partners are in a good situation to be aware of the female's enjoyment and responsivity at this point. The male can be aware of and responsive to his own arousal and that of his partner, and not worried about the state of his erection. It will be the female's initiative to insert his penis into her vagina, in her own time and in her own style. The male is not responsible for pushing or directing this; rather, the responsibility now rests solely with her. If she notices his tension rising or the penis becoming flaccid at any time, she should simply modify her activity until both are feeling comfortable and responsive.

An excellent way to insert the penis is not to make a major step or a major change. Rather than sitting on the penis, lean back on it at about a forty-five degree angle so that it easily makes contact with the vagina. The female guides the insertion with her hand on the penis. If there is any tension or feeling of forced action for either partner, they should simply cease intromission and return to a more comfortable pleasuring position.

After intromission, the female directs the thrusting, and at first she can make the thrusting slow and rhythmic. The tendency is to force the thrusting or make it rapid in order to maintain the erection. However, slow, rhythmic, non-demanding thrusting is probably the best means to maintain an erection, as well as making intercourse both sensual and sexual rather than a performance task. The male can focus on the pleasurable, non-demanding movement and on his awareness of the vaginal warmth and wetness.

If it is mutually desired continue on to orgasm. Again, orgasm occurs as a natural consequence of sexual arousal rather than being striven for or forced. Intercourse should not end abruptly after orgasm. Remember, orgasm does not signal the end of sexual feeling and responsivity. Rather, afterplay or afterglow is as much an integral part of sexual activity as is foreplay and pleasuring.

Most males lose part of their erection within a minute of ejaculation. This is natural and should not cause either partner worry. Some couples enjoy maintaining the intercourse position, and from that position continue caressing, holding, and talking with each other. Other couples prefer to disengage and hold, share feelings, and touch in a different position — sometimes sitting up facing each other or lying side by side, or with one lying on top of the other, etc. Other couples prefer to wash the semen off, while some prefer to lie there and enjoy the feel of the semen. These are individual and couple differences, so find what is most comfortable and sensual for you and share these preferences with your partner. Also, share the fact that in feeling comfortable with responsivity and potency you both will learn to feel comfortable with afterglow, the natural culmination of a pleasurable, mutual sexual experience.

Fourth Set of Exercises For Chapter 8

You have come a long way as a couple in sharing pleasure, feeling comfortable with each other's responsivity, and seeing erections and potency as simply a natural step in the whole process of sexual arousal and responsivity. During the last set of exercises it is important for you as a couple to feel comfortable with some specific techniques to increase responsivity.

Begin the pleasuring in any position you both enjoy. Once you're feeling comfortable and relaxed, the male can rub his flaccid penis against the vulval area of his partner while at the same time using his fingers to caress her in either the genital or non-genital areas. A number of women find this to be quite pleasurable. In the process of doing this and attending to his partner's feelings, the male often becomes aroused and an erection naturally develops. Both partners should also be aware that the woman can respond to manual and flaccid-penile stimulation, and that an erect penis is not necessary to ensure female responsivity. Because of performance anxiety, the male will often avoid initiating sex because he is not sure he will be able to follow through and complete intercourse. For the same reason, he often will not welcome his partner's initiation because he sees it as a demand for sexual performance that he will not be able to meet. Both partners must be comfortable with the fact that every sexual experience does not have to end in intercourse, and that manual and oral stimulation and use of the flaccid penis are all normal and helpful techniques for meeting a female's sexual responsivity. Also, some women feel that they must have an orgasm during intercourse; this puts tremendous pressure on the male and can exacerbate potency problems. It is important for that couple to accept that orgasm achieved by manual, oral, or penis (flaccid or erect) stimulation are all the same and all can be enjoyable and fulfilling.

A fully-erect penis is not always necessary for vaginal intromission. If the male lies on his side and the female lies on her back, leaning slightly toward and facing her partner, she can insert his flaccid or partly-erect penis gently into her vagina, thereby achieving intromission. It's important that the male not try to help her or take the initiative himself, but rather relax and accept his partner's initiative. The female takes the penis with both hands and gently inserts it into her vagina, using pelvic movements and thrusting to increase the pleasurable sensations.

While this is happening the male can be kissing, caressing, and fondling his partner, and simply accepting the intromission. Frequently, at intromission or during penile containment the male finds his arousal level increasing and his erection then naturally becomes harder and more firm.

The important thing in this exercise is for the couple to realize that one does not need a "hard" erection for intromission, and that if there are any problems with intromission, the female can become more active in directing and facilitating the intromission.

If the male has intromission problems, it often happens that he panics and tries to force the penis into the vagina. This usually makes the penis more flaccid, causes the partner discomfort, and frustrates the couple. This is an example of how performance anxiety causes the couple (especially the male) to react in self-defeating ways. The couple needs to accept the fact that increasing responsivity naturally leads to erections and mutual comfort with potency. If the male feels any tension from erectile problems, the female can be helpful by moving a step or two back until he is comfortable and then facilitating arousal and guiding intromission with the soft insertion technique described above.

To end this series of exercises, the couple might attempt intercourse in a position other than female superior. In doing so, allow the stimulation to be more mutual and spontaneous. However, remember that it should not be demanding, but rather building on each other's responsivity. Also, remember the give-to-get principle, and enjoy each other's sexuality rather than worrying or focusing on your own performance. Allow the stimulation to be slow, tender and rhythmic. Don't try to hurry or force arousal. Let intromission be a naturally-occurring event rather than a major hurdle; at this point the male can initiate and guide intromission. However, if he is anxious or tries to force it, his partner should move him a step or two back and she should be more active in facilitating and guiding intromission. Make intercourse itself a mutually sensual, sexual, and satisfying experience rather than something to be accomplished. Be aware of each other's feelings during intercourse and continue to be loving, supportive, and caring of your partner throughout. Spend time in afterplay and afterglow, and again share this feeling of closeness and tenderness. Notice how comfortable you as a couple have become with mutual responsivity and potency.

AFTERWORD

At this point you as a couple should be comfortable in facilitating each other's responsivity and knowing that this naturally leads to erections and potency. Fears about performance anxiety; playing the "spectator role"; feelings of hostility and misunderstanding should now be minimal or totally gone. Does this mean you will never have another experience with not getting or losing an erection? Realistically, you will probably experience potency difficulties from time to time. On occasions of fatigue, high anxiety over money or work, little sex interest, or other circumstances you will undoubtedly feel less sexual, and thus will not be as responsive. You might not have an erection or a hard erection. That does not mean you have a potency problem, unless you start to worry and become anxious again. What it does mean is that at this point, in this situation, you are simply not feeling greatly responsive sexually. You can decide not to have sex that day; or you can decide to use manual, oral, or flaccid-penile methods of sexual arousal with your partner; or you can decide to relax and get into the sexual situation; or you can decide to use the soft insertion technique. You neither have to prove anything, nor do you have to become panicky or worried. As long as you do not fall into the traps of performance anxiety, playing the spectator role, and trying to force an erection, you will probably not have a potency problem. As long as you as a couple continue to work together to facilitate mutual responsivity, you will continue to feel comfortable with potency. You should be pleased with yourselves individually and as a couple, and continue to work to make your sensual and sexual functioning as a couple even more mutually pleasurable.

9 Learning Ejaculatory Control

The myths of performance are among the most powerful negative influences on sexual functioning. For instance, it is a myth that males either do sex well, which is then a sign of masculinity, or they do not know how to be a real man sexually, and are therefore less than masculine. The matter of premature ejaculation is greatly influenced by the performance myths. In reality, the majority of males at some time are premature ejaculators, especially during their early sexual experiences. Many men, as they gain more sexual experience, somehow learn ejaculatory control. However, probably between 20% and 40% of males have trouble with premature ejaculation. In fact, the average time for intercourse (from intromission to ejaculation) among American couples is two minutes.

PREMATURE EJACULATION DEFINED

There is much confusion as to what premature ejaculation is. Some people have defined it in terms of time (thirty seconds after intromission), some in terms of activity (fewer than ten strokes is labeled premature), some in terms of whether the woman is brought to orgasm each time — an extremely poor criterion. The definition used by Masters and Johnson states that if the female is normally orgasmic, premature ejaculation occurs if the male ejaculates before the female's orgasm during 50% of intercourse attempts. Our feeling is that all these definitions are too arbitrary. Rather, a more reasonable approach is that, if the couple is making good use of non-genital and genital foreplay and pleasuring so that the woman is responsive and ready for intercourse, and the male's ejaculation is more rapid than either one of the partners would like, then this is a problem of ejaculatory control. We prefer the term "rapid ejaculation" to "premature ejaculation" and feel that the majority of males could benefit from training in ejaculatory control. Rather than looking at rapid ejaculation as a major sex problem which makes one feel inadequate as a sex partner or makes one's partner feel she is unloved and not cared for, it makes much more sense to think of ejaculatory control as a skill the couple — not just the male — can learn to enhance their mutual sexual functioning.

RAPID EJACULATION

Most males have learned *rapid* ejaculation from a host of cultural and personal experiences, including sex myths which are spread by many sources. Typically, the male's first intercourse might take place in the back seat of a car in a hurried, unplanned way, or on a couch in a woman's house with the fear that her parents might come in, or perhaps with a prostitute who applies a lot of pressure on getting the job done. All these experiences have the common denominator of a good deal of anxiety as well as excitement on the part of the male, along with a special demand to perform rapidly. Also, especially in initial intercourse experiences, the male often is solely concerned with proving himself and reaching orgasm, rather than focusing on his partner's pleasure or even his own pleasure of touching, sensual feelings, and sexual arousal.

An erroneous conception holds that the really "sexy" man can ejaculate very rapidly to show how masculine he is. Often, the male does not see intercourse as a mutual act, but rather as something the male does to the female; in this misconception, her needs and desires are unimportant. Lack of knowledge about sexuality and lack of acceptance of sexuality as being good for the male and the female most often lead to the male's learning to be a rapid ejaculator.

LEARNING EJACULATORY CONTROL

Whatever the specific origin of rapid ejaculation happens to be for a particular male, he can learn ejaculatory control. Working for the sake of a mutually satisfying sexual relationship with his partner, the male can learn ejaculatory control if he and his partner work cooperatively. In the following exercises, the role of the female partner is highly important.

The program for ejaculatory control is built upon the solid foundation you have gained in non-genital and genital touching and pleasuring. In the work with ejaculatory control you will be both giving and receiving pleasure as well as learning a specific technique and skill to control rapid ejaculation.

TRAPS

Before we discuss the ejaculatory-control exercises, another important point deserves mention. Frequently, a male who has labeled himself a premature ejaculator falls into several traps of which he must be aware. One is that often he begins to feel negative about ejaculation. Rather than accepting and enjoying his orgasmic response, he is mentally kicking himself for coming too fast. This negative attitude does not help ejaculatory control in any way. It just makes it possible that the male will begin to avoid sex. This is counterproductive, because the less sex he has, the more likely that his ejaculation will be quite rapid.

DISTRACTIONS

Another trap involves distraction. Many males attempt to rely on various techniques of distraction in a vain effort to postpone the urge to ejaculate. For example, during intromission and intercourse some males might try to think of work to be done, a TV program seen recently, or an athletic event. Or, perhaps they might attempt physical distraction such as clenching a fist, biting a lip, pinching themselves, etc. Other males have attempted to put an anesthetizing cream on the head of the penis, to wear two or three condoms, etc. — all in vain attempts to delay the feelings of ejaculatory inevitability. These activities are all essentially counterproductive, since in "distracting" himself in order to delay orgasm, the male is more importantly distracting himself from the sensual, pleasurable feelings of touch, arousal, and intercourse. Thus inadvertently he is learning to tune out some of his positive sexual feelings. Often, the female partner feels neglected or rejected by the resulting lack of male excitement. This often leads to a general decline in her sexual arousal, and negative feelings toward her partner in turn. All distracting strategies are based on the same premise: that it is solely the male's responsibility to control his ejaculation and that the best way to do this is to avoid thinking about arousal or having his penis touched or stimulated. That premise and those strategies only add to the problems.

SHARED RESPONSIBILITIES

The exercises and approach you will learn here are based on the principle that learning ejaculatory control is a responsibility of both partners. The best way to develop ejaculatory control is to take an active, direct approach to the penis, utilizing the squeeze technique.

You should read this chapter separately and then sit down and discuss it. Remember, ejaculatory control is important to you both. It requires the active participation and support of both partners. Most important of all, it requires persistence. You will learn two key things: where the point of ejaculatory inevitability is, and how to increase the time from arousal to ejaculation.

Sexual arousal is a naturally occurring, voluntary response in the male up to the point of ejaculatory inevitability; at this point, ejaculation becomes an involuntary response, i.e., the male will ejaculate even if he tries to stop it. If the squeeze technique is utilized *before* the point of ejaculatory inevitability, it retards the urge to ejaculate. What then happens is that the male gradually learns to maintain his sexual arousal without feeling the urge to ejaculate. When he is consistently able to maintain sexual arousal without ejaculating, we say the couple has learned ejaculatory control.

First Set of Exercises For Chapter 9

First talk about the positive feelings and experiences you have had with non-genital and genital pleasuring. You have learned how to give and receive feedback. You will need to use this capacity along with the ability to work cooperatively. Discuss your feelings about working as a cooperative couple to learn ejaculatory control.

As a natural continuation of the genital pleasuring exercises, arrange yourselves in a position where the female leans back comfortably with her back supported by a pillow or cushion against the bed's headboard. The male positions his body comfortably between his partner's spread legs, lying on his back facing his partner, with his legs bent in a comfortable manner and resting on the mattress outside his partner's thigh region. It is important that you both feel comfortable and relaxed in this position.

Once in a comfortable position, the female begins

massaging the male's chest and then slowly and naturally works down to his genital area. She utilizes stroking and fondling movements she has found comfortable to give, and to which he responds sexually and sensually. As his arousal increases, he will naturally get an erection. A few moments after a hard erection is achieved, the female should apply the squeeze technique to her partner's penis. She can do this by placing her thumb just behind the glans (at the underside) with two fingers near the coronal ridge. The forefinger is near the coronal ridge, and the middle finger about an inch down on the shaft. (See Figure 11) With the thumb and fingers thus positioned, the female should squeeze hard for about fifteen to twenty seconds, or until the male begins to lose his erection.

Figure 11

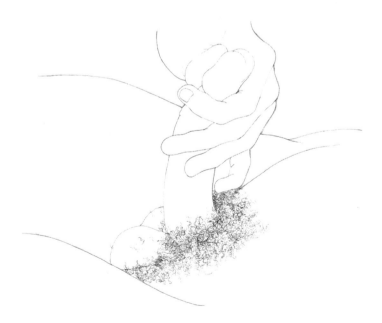

Often there is a tendency not to squeeze hard because of fear of hurting the male. As soon as the penis is erect, however, one can squeeze it very hard without causing pain. If at any point the squeezing were to become painful, then the male would signal. The female should not be afraid to squeeze hard and vigorously; this is very important in learning ejaculatory control.

Typically, after the squeeze has been applied to the penis, the male loses both the urge to ejaculate and also part of his erection — one would say about half of the effect of the erection. This happens because the blood flow to the penis is interrupted, and also because the arousing stimulation has been stopped temporarily.

At first, the female will probably begin squeezing well before the male has the urge to ejaculate. This early squeezing is all right; it will give both partners practice in using the squeeze technique. It will take practice and feedback to get used to the technique; however, many couples do find it pleasing and sensual. At the very least we hope that you will find it comfortable.

After about ten seconds the female again returns to sensual and sexually arousing fondling and manual stimulation. She should not concentrate all her time on the penis. Rather, she should massage the stomach, teasingly play with the testicles, and run her fingers along the inner thigh, making it enjoyable and sensuous for herself. The male should simply accept the sensual and sexual feelings. He should not concentrate on getting an erection; instead, he should just allow it to happen. If, after a squeeze, he does not regain an erection, neither partner should worry; instead, both should just enjoy the sensual feelings.

Frequently the male who has difficulty with rapid ejaculation down not want to focus on the pleasurable feelings in his penis because he is afraid that these feelings will overly excite him and he will ejaculate. Using the squeeze technique, he should focus on and accept these pleasurable feelings. He should also be aware of his mounting sexual arousal so that he can learn to be a better discriminator of his sexual excitement, especially as he approaches the point of ejaculatory inevitability. He should be aware of and accept the sexual feelings that precede the feeling of ejaculatory inevitability. Discriminating these feelings is a crucial beginning step in learning ejaculatory control.

It is important that the couple develop a mutually agreed-upon communication system to signal when to utilize the squeeze. Some common signals are the male saying "now"; raising one hand; saying "squeeze," or taping her hand. The male must signal *before* he reaches the point of ejaculatory inevitability, and the female must squeeze immediately.

Use the stimulation and squeeze technique for at least twenty minutes and up to thirty minutes. There will usually be at least three squeezes during this time. The first time, the woman should initiate the squeeze early in the arousal cycle; the second time, after he has had the erection for about thirty seconds; the third time, after forty-five seconds. The male should be aware of his heightened arousal. If he feels any urge to ejaculate, he should tell his partner *immediately* so she can use the squeeze. However, if the male should ejaculate, neither partner should feel upset or guilty. This is a perfectly normal consequence and both partners should enjoy the ejaculation.

When you both feel comfortable with the basic techniques of ejaculatory control, the enjoyable stimulation, and the use of the squeeze technique, then you have done well. At this point, the female partner deserves to be the recipient of pleasuring. If you have decided to work on the program to increase female responsivity, you should begin those exercises at this point. If you are not working on specific exercises, the the female partner should simply guide the male in the type of non-genital or genital pleasuring that she finds particularly sensual or sexually arousing.

The male partner should allow himself to be actively involved in and enjoying the pleasuring experience.

When the pleasuring is completed you might want to get dressed and, over a drink or coffee, openly share the feelings about the utilization of the squeeze technique and cooperatively working toward learning ejaculatory control.

Second Set of Exercises For Chapter 9

For this exercise, at first postpone the stimulation-squeeze procedure. Instead, do some affectionate, playful, and enjoyable pleasuring first. Then change to the ejaculatory control position previously described. The male should be in a comfortable position lying on his back, with his legs stretched out flat against the bed. The female partner should position herself so that she has full access to his genitals.

Begin the stimulation technique by directly massaging and caressing the penis in the most stimulating manner possible to bring him closer and closer to the point of ejaculatory inevitably. At this point, use manual rather than oral-genital stimulation. One very effective technique is to use one hand on the penis, and simultaneously to lift the testicles in a teasing manner or massage the stomach or run your fingers over the pubic hair with the other hand.

When the male feels he is approaching the point of ejaculatory inevitability, he should signal his partner to employ the squeeze technique, squeezing hard for fifteen to twenty seconds until he loses the urge to ejaculate and partially loses his erection.

Since the male is learning to discriminate the point of ejaculatory inevitability, he will probably signal late at least once or twice and will ejaculate. Do not worry about this. It is quite natural and is important in learning discrimination. Also, the male should enjoy the feeling of ejaculation rather than being angry or disappointed with himself. The female should also accept the ejaculation rather than feeling frustrated with her partner or with herself for not doing the squeeze in time. To learn ejaculatory control takes practice, mistakes, and cooperation. If the male has ejaculated you can move to female pleasuring and then end the session, or if you are interested and desire to, you can then return to the penile stimulation and squeeze procedure.

If an ejaculation does not occur, the female should keep up stimulation for at least twenty minutes. Do this even if you must use twenty squeezes! After each squeeze, allow the erection to decrease, wait fifteen to twenty seconds, and begin restimulation. Squeeze hard enough to reduce the erection. You should use a variety of stimulation techniques, and be aware of and enjoy the responsivity of your partner. After twenty to thirty minutes you might want to then carry the stimulation on to orgasm for the male. Then reverse roles and allow the female to enjoy accepting and responding to the pleasure, with the male utilizing his unique style of pleasuring his partner.

You might want to repeat this exercise several times. In subsequent attempts, you might use Vaseline to lubricate the penis. The sensations are somewhat similar to those during intercourse, when the penis is in contact with a lubricated vagina. Be sure that the male can discriminate and identify the point of ejaculatory inevitability and the female can use the squeeze to retard the urge to ejaculate. The male should really focus on, and allow himself to enjoy, the feelings in his penis before ejaculatory inevitability. It is important that these skills be mastered before moving on to the next set of exercises. Be sure you are both confident and working together before moving on.

Third Set of Exercises For Chapter 9

Now that you have learned the basic techniques of ejaculatory

control, you may utilize them in an intercourse context. The best
intercourse position in which to practice ejaculatory control is female
superior. This is a very good position both for ejaculatory control
and for increasing female activity and response. (See Figure 12)
The male lies on his back, with his legs stretched out flat against the
bed. The female partner lies over him with her knees at his chest so
that her vulval area is adjacent to his genital area. She rests her
buttocks on his thigh region. From this position the female can
manually stimulate the penis as well as rubbing the penis around the
clitoris and the labia minora. She may also run it around the vaginal
opening, but she should not insert it. When the male feels close to
the point of ejaculatory inevitability, he should signal his partner
immediately to use the squeeze.

Figure 12

This exercise will continue for at least twenty minutes and up to forty minutes. Use the squeeze as often as necessary; it is important, if possible, to include at least three squeezes. Again, if the male does ejaculate, simply accept it and enjoy it. Remember, you are learning to discriminate the point of ejaculatory inevitability as well as to elongate the time between arousal and ejaculation. Doing these things will take practice and supportive feedback.

Another valuable stimulation technique with which the female can experiment is use of her breasts, if she feels confortable doing so. She can begin by rubbing his penis around each breast in a gentle and sensuous manner. Then she can put his penis in the crevice between the breasts, and if she has large breasts, bring her breasts together and move them up and down while encircling the penis. This partly simulates the feeling and movement of the vagina, and many males find it quite arousing. When he feels the urge to ejaculate, she should use the squeeze.

In the female superior position, the couple has the advantage of easier mutual pleasuring. The male can be massaging and touching his partner while she is doing the penile stimulation. Also, the female should allow herself to accept and enjoy the feelings of sensuousness and arousal as she rubs the penis around her clitoris, labia, and vagina. At the end, the male should engage in some enjoyable pleasuring of his partner, and she should allow herself to bask in feelings of sensuousness and sexuality. Both might want to proceed to manual, oral or intercourse means to attain orgasm for one or both partners.

It might be necessary to repeat this set of exercises until both of you are sure that you have developed good ejaculatory control in sexually-arousing, non-intercourse positions. You might sit and talk about your feelings of accomplishment and pleasure as you continue to work together and gain greater ejaculatory control.

Fourth Set of Exercises For Chapter 9

During this set of exercises you will again be utilizing the female superior position. The female should begin by using gentle stroking of her partner's face and chest, then move to manual stimulation of the penis, and finally to rubbing the penis around the clitoris and vagina. After the first utilization of the squeeze, restimulate the penis until it becomes erect. As soon as it becomes erect, the female should guide the penis by placing it in at about a forty-five degree angle and sliding back on it. After intromission, simply remain still; just allow the penis to remain in the vagina. This part of the exercise is called the quiet vagina. The male should make no movement; he should just enjoy the feeling of intravaginal containment. He should focus on the warm, sensual feelings of his penis being contained in his partner's vagina. The female can find this feeling to be particularly arousing; she should stay with and accept the feeling but avoid any rapid thrusting. She should move slowly and non-demandingly, and use only enough movement to insure that the male does not lose his erection.

If at any point the male feels the point of ejaculatory inevitability, he should signal the female to break the coital connection by lifting herself up and off the penis. She should use the squeeze technique. She should then stimulate to erection, again initiate intromission, and maintain intercourse for at least twenty minutes — longer if both prefer. The quiet vagina should be repeated at least once at a later time. The next step involves intromission in the female superior position, but instead of no movement, the female initiates a gentle, slow, and non-demanding thrusting. Again, when the male feels a need to ejaculate he signals, she breaks coital connection, squeezes, restimulates, and again initiates intromission and slow movement. As with the other exercises the couple is encouraged to repeat this exercise a few times; each repetition increases the ejaculatory control. Remember, ejaculatory control is learned gradually and requires continued practice.

The next steps are:

1. The male initiates slow, gentle, non-demanding thrusting.
2. The female initiates more rapid, demanding thrusting.
3. The male initiates more rapid, demanding thrusting.

In practicing each of these steps, remember to use the squeeze technique each time when necessary. If ejaculation occurs, accept and enjoy it. At each step try for at least twenty minutes of intravaginal containment without ejaculation; do this even if you have to use the squeeze many times. Each step should be repeated at least twice, and you might want to repeat it several times. Each repetition will teach you as a couple to be more comfortable with ejaculatory control. You will find you will need to use the squeeze technique less and less often. In fact, you might want to use a variant of the squeeze technique: simply stopping movement, but keeping the penis in the vagina. When the need to ejaculate disappears, you can then begin movement again.

After you have reached the goal of ejaculatory control for at least twenty minutes of intravaginal containment, you might then want to go on to complete intercourse to ejaculation. Either the female or male may signal her or his partner, and if the partner agrees you may proceed to complete intercourse. This should be a mutual decision, and neither should feel pressure to complete intercourse each time. At this point, we would suggest you continue to utilize the female superior position to ejaculation. Both of you should allow yourselves to enjoy the intercourse and ejaculation. After the exercise or intercourse is completed, do not simply break contact, but rather engage in afterplay or afterglow. Share with each other the warm, intimate feelings of the experience you have just completed. Sex does not end with the end of intercourse. Sharing the afterglow is very important. Realize and share how far you as a couple have come not only in learning ejaculatory control, but also in learning how to be a mutually loving and sexual couple.

AFTERWORD

Learning ejaculatory control is like learning any other skill. It occurs gradually, takes time and practice, and requires feedback. You will probably want to practice that fourth set of exercises for at least a couple of weeks before moving on to other intercourse positions. When you do move on, you should know that male superior is the most difficult of all the intercourse positions in terms of ejaculatory control. One of the best both in terms of ejaculatory control and mutual sexual responsivity is the lateral coital position. (Refer to the third set of exercises, Chapter 13.)

You will probably be using the squeeze technique to some extent for between six months and a year. It will be especially important to use it when you and your partner are having intercourse after a break of several days. Do not be afraid to use the squeeze technique as often as necessary. Remember to continue to discuss your experience and give feedback to your partner as you progress together in feeling more sure of and comfortable with ejaculatory control.

10 Increasing Enjoyment of Oral-Genital Stimulation

Through the pleasuring exercises, you and your partner have become increasingly aware and appreciative of your capacity for sensual and sexual pleasure in both the non-genital and genital areas of your body. As you have become more aware, you have found that you are less likely to feel embarrassed and inhibited about the exploration of either your own body or your partner's. Acceptance and comfort have replaced past feelings of tension, guilt, and misunderstanding. You have learned to be positive in recognizing, feeling, and accepting your sexuality, and in accepting yourselves as a sensuous, sexual, and loving couple.

However, because of personal and cultural expectations, there might be a tendency to partition off certain types of sexual expression and arousal. More specifically, some couples might enjoy and accept all types of touch including genital touch and might enjoy kissing and oral stimulation of non-genital areas, but might bypass or actively avoid kissing and orally stimulating their partner's genital region. However, for many couples oral-genital stimulation is a highly pleasant component of sexual expression and sexual arousal. Just as one learns to feel pleasure from kissing and other forms of oral stimulation to non-genital areas, one can learn to extend the pleasuring to the genital areas and find it quite exciting.

Quite possibly, negative attitudes toward oral-genital stimulation are an outgrowth of the mistaken notion that the genitals are "dirty" in a physical sense. Since the penis is used both for urination and ejaculation some people mistakenly associate these two functions. In reality, they are separate functions; when sexually aroused, a male cannot and will not urinate. At times, during stimulation, a small amount of liquid seeps out of the penis. This can be either a secretion from the Cowper's gland or semen, not urination; it is perfectly normal. This liquid can be tasted and swallowed with no harmful effects. Similarly, the vulval area is physically close to the urethra and also somewhat close to the anus — but again, the functions are completely different. The female secretion during sexual arousal comes from the vagina. It is not urine. Vaginal secretion can also be tasted and swallowed with no harmful effects. In fact, many males and females find the smell and taste of vaginal secretion and semen to be quite pleasurable and arousing.

It is important that your personal hygiene be extended to the genital area so that it is as clean as other parts of your body.

At times, during oral stimulation, loose pubic hair might get into your mouth. This is not bad or unusual; simply remove it. While some people are responsive to the sexual stimulation of pubic hair, others are not. For these latter people, one might try some method of hair removal. A typical pattern is for the female to leave the hair on the mons area intact, and to remove all posterior hair beginning at the labia. This can be accomplished quite easily with a commercial depilatory cream, after testing for allergic reactions. The soft smooth surface of the labia after the removal of the hair is very pleasant. Removing labial hair may also reduce odor in this area.

MORAL JUDGMENTS

Some people have mistakenly learned that oral-genital stimulation is a form of so-called perversion. Along the same lines, there is a widespread myth that oral genital stimulation is practiced exclusively by homosexuals or that it is a sign of latent homosexuality. Although some homosexuals do engage in oral-genital sex, the behavior happens to be homosexual simply because members of the same sex might engage in it. (In other words, any sexual behavior is "homosexual" or "heterosexual," depending entirely upon whether same-sex or male-female partners engage in it.) Oral-genital stimulation is a perfectly normal and acceptable form of heterosexual activity. In fact, rather than a perversion, oral-genital stimulation has been found to be used and enjoyed by the majority of well-adjusted, well-functioning heterosexual couples. Oral-genital stimulation adds to the couple's feelings of sexual pleasure, acceptance and arousal. It is simply one more pleasuring technique that can enhance feelings of sensuality and sexuality.

As with the other exercises, we suggest you read these separately and then discuss them. The exercises are intended to last forty-five to ninety minutes, but follow your own pace. Remember, in doing the exercises it is vitally important that communication, both verbal and non-verbal, be open and honest. Also, remember that rather than being goal-oriented, you should focus on learning and exploring. First be aware of and understand your own feelings and reactions, so you can share those with your partner.

First Set of Exercises For Chapter 10

Begin with a relaxing and sensual bath or shower. Let your partner wash you, including your genital area. Be sure that your partner is thorough so that you feel clean. Teach your partner how to wash you so that you are as clean as you would like to be. Remember that as the genitals are an integral part of your body, you should take the same time and care in washing them as you do your face and legs.

In beginning the pleasuring, use the same techniques of integrating genital and non-genital touch that you have used previously. Remember not to focus immediately on genital touching. A good guideline is that at least half of the attention and touching should be oriented toward non-genital areas. Typically, the first time the pleasurer will be the female unless you as a couple decide that the male needs to develop more comfort in giving genital pleasure. The pleasuree should keep his eyes closed and be receptive to learning new feelings and responses.

The pleasurer should begin with touch, using not only her hands but also body contact: using her forearms to touch his chest, rubbing her legs against his, or draping her hair over his face and neck. The male will be lying comfortably on his back, with the female in a kneeling or half-sitting position so her movements can be flexible and she can have good access to her partner's body.

In gliding your hands over your partner's genital area, pause and notice the texture of the skin and pubic hair. While examining and visually exploring, gently trace the borders of the pubic hair and then glide your fingers through it. Next, move back to the non-genital areas and comfortably explore the various types of non-genital oral stimulation you like best — kissing, gliding your tongue over the body, taking gentle love bites, sucking, or any other oral technique you enjoy. Then you might try outlining the pubic area by kissing or tongue-gliding around the entire area from the navel to the thighs. As much as possible, be sensitive to your partner's reactions. If you or your partner begin to feel uncomfortable or tense during the exercise, simply back up a step or two until you feel more comfortable. Don't worry about this or let yourself become upset. For many of us the cultural taboo against oral activity around the genitals is strong. Simply accept the fact that you and your partner will need to proceed at your own pace to develop a mutually acceptable and comfortable approach to oral-genital stimulation. There are no right patterns. It is a matter of the couple finding what is acceptable, fun, and good for them.

Continue the kissing and other oral sensual stimulation until you are at the point where you feel comfortable in giving oral stimulation near the genital area. At this point, do not directly stimulate the genital region itself orally. Instead, manually stimulate your partner's genitals in the way you have learned is most sensually and sexually arousing, while at the same time orally stimulating all around the genital area. When you and your partner feel comfortable in giving and receiving the oral stimulation, then switch roles and repeat the process with the male using his unique style as pleasurer.

When you have completed the exercises, perhaps you could sit nude in bed (or if it is more comfortable, get dressed) and over coffee or a drink share feelings about giving and receiving oral stimulation.

Second Set of Exercises For Chapter 10

During this set of exercises your eyes can be open so that you will feel free to use eye contact in the communication process. The man will start as pleasurer unless the couple has decided otherwise.

As a natural progression from the first set of exercises, you again explore your partner's body with manual and oral stimulation by the female as pleasuree and male as pleasurer. This time the pleasuree will guide her partner.

Teach him the kind of oral stimulation you find

most sensuous and most sexually pleasing. Do not be afraid to encourage your partner to try new kinds of stimulation.

Approaching the vulval area, continue with the sensual kisses at the outline of her pubic hair. Then gradually and comfortably kiss the inside portions of her thighs, while at the same time using your hands to stroke or glide across the outer portions of her thighs, buttocks, and lower back. Then while continuing to stimulate orally around the vulval area, use your hands and fingers to stimulate her genitals manually. Be aware of her reactions, particularly whether she is relaxed, lubricating, and responsive. At this point both you and your partner should be fairly comfortable with oral stimulation around the vulval area. If not, simply continue oral stimulation or perhaps move back a step until both you and your partner are comfortable. At each exercise you will feel more relaxed and more positive; remember to be in tune with the feelings of yourself and your partner and go at your own pace. All the while the pleasurer is doing this he should be getting comfortable with the visual exploration of the vulval area.

At this point the pleasuree should shut her eyes and tune in to her new feelings and experiences when her partner begins oral stimulation of her vulval area. In orally stimulating the vulval area for the first time you might begin with tongue movements around her labia minora. Then insert the tip of your tongue between the labia minora, using darting tongue movements with slight pauses. Also, you might try sensually caressing the labia minora with your lips. Then move your kissing to the clitoral area. Try using a gentle sucking motion around the clitoris. This area is very sensitive, so remember to be gentle. Be aware of the texture and sensations as your tongue touches the clitoris and around the clitoral shaft. Be sure that you are aware of your own and your partner's feelings. Remember, if at any time you or your partner become uncomfortable or anxious simply move back a step. Sometimes when aroused the clitoris is so sensitive that it is painful, so it is critical that you stay in touch with your partner's level of arousal. Next move down to the vaginal area. First, simply run your tongue around the outside of the vagina and be especially aware of the taste of the vaginal secretions. It is safe and clean, and many males find the taste and smell to be highly arousing sexually. Be aware of your feelings so you can share them verbally with your partner afterward.

You might then kiss the vaginal area, and while doing so run your tongue around the vaginal opening. Then kiss the vagina and bring the vaginal folds into your mouth. Remember, provide your partner with a variety of forms of oral stimulation so that she might be aware of differences in pressure and discover what she finds most sensuous and sexually arousing. In continuing the vulval exploration, move up to the mons area and glide your tongue through the pubic hair. What is the sensation of moving through the hair? Again, many men and women find this particularly sexually arousing; be open to your feelings and reactions. Then run your tongue from the tip of the clitoral shaft to the vagina, and kiss and suck in those areas. The pleasurer should continue until he feels he has given his partner a variety of oral stimulation experiences. At this point, the pleasurer should be tuned into learning about the vulval area, the types of oral stimulation his partner responds to, what is sensual and what is sexually arousing. When this part of the exercise is completed, rather than stopping abruptly, return to non-genital oral stimulation and end the experience with a loving and tender kiss on the lips.

Then switch roles, with the female being pleasurer. At first the pleasuree's eyes should be open and he should be guiding his partner in the oral stimulation around his genitals. In moving toward his pubic-genital area, you might again outline the area with erotic, sensual kisses. Simultaneously, you might use your hands to massage and stroke across his abdomen and thighs. Continue with the sensual kisses and tongue movements until you have reached the inside portion of his thighs. As you orally stimulate this area, manually stimulate the genital region and penis in the sensuous and sexually arousing ways you have learned in the genital touching exercises. Be sure you are comfortable with oral stimulation close to the genitals before moving on to the next step. Remember to move at your own pace rather than pressuring or pushing yourself.

In beginning the oral stimulation of your partner's genital area, hold the penis at the shaft and first visually examine the penis while you are gently stroking and caressing it. Then you might try tongue movement at the glans area of the penis, perhaps punctuating tongue-darting with soft sweeping motions, using only your tongue. Then caress the glans with your lips, while continuing to stroke the penile shaft and frenulum with your hand. Next kiss the entire penis from the shaft to the head. When you get to the head, gently squeeze the tip together with two fingers. You might notice a drop of semen come forth. Remember, semen is safe. (In fact, it is full of protein.) During sex play and sexual arousal, urinary functions never come into play. You might take the small drop of semen and notice how it feels and how it smells. You might also put it on the tip of your tongue and notice how it tastes. At this point, do not put the penis in your mouth, but do experiment with a variety of types of stimulation which allow you to explore your partner's genital area orally. This exploration allows him to be aware of a variety of types of stimulation techniques so that he might learn what types are most sensual and sexually arousing for him. Later, he will be guiding you and sharing his learning with you. Remember that there are no right or wrong responses, and the goal is to learn what types of oral stimulation and pleasuring each of you enjoys giving and receiving. Thus, it is important to be aware of your own feelings and responsiveness, as well as the responsiveness and feelings of your partner.

Before ending this exercise you might explore his

scrotum area and testicles. Look at, touch, and then gently kiss and suck on his testicles — be aware which is larger and what the shapes are like. If you happen to get any hair in your mouth, it is nothing to be concerned about — simply remove it. Be aware of the sensation of the hair and the scent of the genital area. You might end the exploration by running your tongue over the entire penis, noticing which parts are particularly attractive. However, don't devote all your attention to the penis. Interchange manual and oral stimulation on the thighs, stomach, and sides.

If at any time you or your partner become again uncomfortable, do not be upset about it. Simply move back a step or two until you are comfortable with oral stimulation of the penis, and you feel you have given your partner a variety of experiences. Then you might spend a minute or so kissing each other on the lips, face, and neck. Afterward, discuss the one or two things that you found most arousing about receiving oral-genital stimulation. Also discuss your feelings about giving oral stimulation, particularly what you found most enjoyable about it. If there were unenjoyable or anxiety-provoking aspects, discuss these, and talk about how you can learn to be more comfortable with them, or how to substitute more comfortable oral or manual stimulation.

Third Set of Exercises For Chapter 10

These exercises should be done with eyes open so that you are more aware and more accepting of your partner as you give oral stimulation. The pleasuree should also guide the partner in teaching both the pattern of oral stimulation which is most sexually arousing and new oral-genital stimulation procedures that he or she would like to experience.

The pleasuree the first time should be the male, unless you as a couple feel that the female needs to develop more comfort in receiving pleasure. This time, try a different position for oral pleasuring. Lying across the bed, the male can be comfortably positioned on his side with his head facing the head of the bed. The female can lie comfortably on her side with her head facing the foot of the bed. For her own ease, she should position herself so that both her hands and mouth have comfortable and easy access to the male's genitals. (See. Figure 13)

Begin the pleasuring by stimulating the penis orally. Then move to manual genital stimulation, and then oral and manual non-genital stimulation. Notice the differences in feelings as you do this, and be aware that being comfortable in oral-genital stimulation does not mean that you must concentrate on it solely. Return to oral-genital stimulation, and let your partner guide you and teach you the type of oral stimulation he finds most enjoyable.

Figure 13

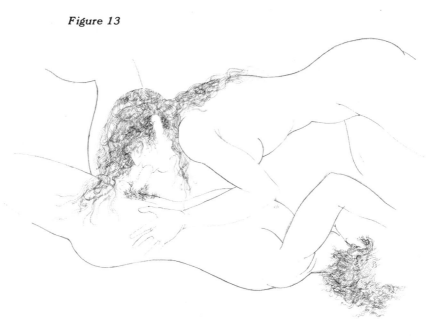

You might then try some new oral stimulation techniques. Many people find that deep oral contact, with the penis placed deeply into the mouth, is quite exciting. Some women hesitate to do this, even when they want to experience it, because of the gagging response one gets when anything goes deeply into one's mouth. You can prevent this by two means. One is to put the penis in on an angle so that it touches the side of the mouth rather than the back of the throat. The second is to put the penis directly into your mouth, but to keep your hand clasped around the shaft of the penis when you are making deep oral enclosures. This gives you greater control and more contact, as well as eliminating the chance of your partner thrusting too deeply into your throat, which could cause you discomfort. With both techniques be sure to wrap your lips around your teeth, since the penis is sensitive and contact with the teeth could cause soreness.

When the penis is in your mouth, experiment with movement directed by you as compared to movement directed by him. Most couples use in-and-out movements, but you might want to experiment with circular movement in the mouth, tongue-kissing with the penis in the mouth, or very gently touching the penis with the teeth. Notice the taste of secretions from the penis. Many women find this quite sensuous. Be aware of and responsive to your partner's reactions. There is a difference in style among couples as to whether they want to use oral techniques to orgasm or not. There is no normal or right response; it is strictly a matter of individual preference. Some couples enjoy oral-genital relations strictly as a pleasuring or foreplay technique, not culminating in orgasm. Others enjoy the experience culminating in orgasm, at least occasionally. If you want to experiment with the latter, there are two styles: the first, where the male ejaculates into his partner's mouth, and the second where they separate and he ejaculates onto the bed or onto her body. (Often she will use additional manual stimulation to bring him to orgasm.) If you prefer, try receiving the ejaculate in the mouth. Remember, the semen is perfectly safe and germ-free. The taste of the ejaculate is very similar to the taste of the penis before ejaculation. Be aware of the scent and taste and your feelings about it. Many women feel this is a lovely way to gain further acceptance of their partner.

Another stylistic choice — remember, there are no right or wrong responses, but only knowing what sexually feels comfortable to you — is whether the woman wants to swallow the ejaculate or to spit it out on the bed or on a tissue or towel.

End this part of the exercise when both you and your partner feel comfortable with your own style of mouth-penis contact. You will probably want to do this exercise often to establish your style; the most important thing is that it is your own style, which you can use to express love and affection, and with which you can enhance your sexuality. Spend some time holding and kissing each other, and then switch pleasuring roles.

The male should repeat the same sequence of orally stimulating the vulval area, then moving to manual genital stimulation, then oral and manual non-genital stimulation, and then finally to oral-genital stimulation with his partner guiding him. He should be a receptive learner.

Next, explore deeper types of oral stimulation. Try a different technique for clitoral stimulation. Begin with tongue-gliding around the clitoral shaft, and then gently kiss and suck on the clitoris until you feel your partner becoming quite aroused. Remember to be sensitive to her reactions and responses, making it sensuous and exciting for her, but not painful. Move down the labia minora, using tongue, kissing, and sucking movements. Very gently kiss and caress the vaginal opening until there is a good deal of vaginal secretion, and notice the taste and smell of the secretions, using them to increase your own feelings of sensuousness.

Next kiss and suck on the vagina, allowing your tongue to go into the vagina. Then concentrate on kissing, sucking, and caressing the clitoral shaft and the labia minora. Many women find this the most sensuous and sexually arousing form of oral stimulation. Again, be aware of your partner's responses and follow her guidance.

The question of whether oral-genital stimulation should be used strictly as a pleasuring or foreplay technique or also as an orgasmic outlet is more complex for females than for males. Again, there are no right or wrong responses; it is a matter of the couple's style and feelings. Since a woman is able to have several orgasms, it is entirely possible and it often occurs that she can be orgasmic with oral stimulation and then be orgasmic during intercourse. In fact, having an orgasmic foreplay will often make it easier to be orgasmic during intercourse for a multiorgasmic women. Therefore, many couples do decide to carry oral stimulation through to orgasm. If you decide to continue through to orgasm, remember that an orgasm is simply a natural response to steady, rhythmic, and direct oral stimulation. Allow your partner to develop her own rhythm of sexual responsivity and simply follow this rhythm, letting it evolve as you continue with pleasurable and consistent oral stimulation. If you decide to use oral-genital stimulation only as a pleasuring or foreplay technique you can either go on to intercourse or gradually allow the arousal level to subside by not stopping the oral stimulation abruptly but rather making it less intense and allowing your partner to return slowly and comfortably to a pleasant sensual state. Be aware of her feelings and make the post-arousal period as enjoyable and sensual for her as possible by continuing pleasuring which is not sexually arousing.

This exercise can be stopped when you are both feeling comfortable with the breadth and depth of your oral-genital stimulation. You might end by hugging and kissing, and while lying in bed explore your feelings about use of oral-genital stimulation as a pleasuring or foreplay technique as compared to a technique which is oriented toward orgasm. Oral-genital stimulation can be used for different purposes at different times and in different situations if you so desire. It is a natural and positive technique that you as a couple can use to enhance your sensual and sexual pleasure.

Fourth Set of Exercises For Chapter 10

In this set of exercises there are two main considerations. One is to integrate your feelings about oral-genital stimulation: to make it a more mutual experience and to include it as one part of your other ways of giving and receiving pleasure. The second is to experiment with mutual oral-genital stimulation. Colloquially, this is known as "sixty-nine" and often is the topic of jokes and risque comments. It is a perfectly normal and healthy expression of sexual feelings. Many couples find it immensely pleasurable. The exercises should be done with eyes open, using direct and immediate responsive communication to increase your comfort.

Begin the exercises lying side-by-side facing each other. Start with non-genital touch, using both manual and oral stimulation. Then naturally and comfortably move into genital touch, interchanging manual and oral stimulation. Allow the manual and oral stimulation to complement each other. Give feedback as you allow the process to flow. Sometimes one will be more active and initiating, sometimes the other, and often there will be a mutual giving and receiving pleasure. Be aware of your own unique style as a couple and integrate what you have learned in the oral-genital stimulation to a give-and-take foreplay experience. Remember the give-to-get principle. That is, arousing the responsivitity of your partner is often the most enjoyable of all sexual techniques. Be aware of your own and your partner's responses, go with them and enhance them. If your partner does something that makes you uncomfortable, do not just say no or push your partner away. Instead, give suggestions or guidance toward some activity that would give you pleasure. This is one of the most important of all the principles of effective sexual functioning: Instead of saying no, say yes to something more pleasurable.

If you are comfortable in a more spontaneous, mutual pleasuring experience where oral-genital stimulation is integrated with non-genital and genital touch, then you should move on to experiment with mutual oral-genital stimulation. (See Figure 14) Simply utilize your learning and experience about what your partner enjoys and what you enjoy doing and do it at the same time your partner is stimulating you. Note: Sometimes as one partner becomes aroused, the stimulation techniques become too rough (i.e., the male sucking too hard, or the female rubbing her teeth on the penis). If this happens, the partner should immediately communicate that he or she wants more gentleness.

Figure 14

Some couples enjoy simultaneous mutual stimulation, while others would rather have one orally stimulated while the other is either passive or using manual stimulation. Again, explore and enjoy your responses and continue to develop your own unique style as a couple.

When you are feeling comfortable with your developing style, you can end this group of exercises, but do not forget the importance of afterglow. This is a warm, intimate holding and sharing at the end of the sexual experience which is an integral part of your functioning as a loving and sexually responsive couple.

AFTERWORD

In discovering the pleasuring of giving and receiving oral-genital stimulation, you have added to your own acceptance of your sexuality as well as enhancing your sexual functioning as a couple. You have found that, rather than oral sex being dirty or abnormal, it can very much enhance your sensual and sexual functioning. The majority of well-functioning sexual couples do use and enjoy oral-genital stimulation. Now you can continue to share and give feedback as you develop your own unique style of enjoying oral-genital stimulation. It is another experience to be integrated into your view of yourself as a healthy, sensual and sexual person and your functioning as a loving couple.

11 Increasing Comfort with Non-Demand Pleasuring

One of the most widely believed and harmful myths that keeps a couple from achieving tenderness and spontaneous feeling for each other is the belief that every touching or other affectionate experience must and should end in intercourse. One of the most crippling aspects of marital sex is the notion that the couple cannot just tease or be affectionate or be close, but that any physical intimacy is an invitation to intercourse. This notion makes spontaneous feelings of touching and pleasure into a demand for a more intimate experience.

It is our feeling that spontaneity and sharing would increase if partners were free to share their feelings and touch without an expectancy and demand being placed on them for a payoff (i.e., orgasm) other than simply the enjoyment of being together. In other words, you as a couple can and should be able to enjoy touching and pleasuring in a non-demanding atmosphere.

Our feeling is that sensual and sexual pleasure and experience are enhanced if partners can be free and comfortable in their expression, without feeling that each contact must end in intercourse or orgasm. In fact, we suggest that whenever they feel a need to be close to their partner, a couple could engage in pleasuring which is sensual but does not end in intercourse.

SHARING PLEASING THOUGHTS

Most of the demands in a sexual experience exist because people do not share with each other how they feel about being together — how much they enjoy just being close and affectionate when they just want to be playful and nothing more. If the sexual interaction is based on the myth that in order for the experience to be satisfying the couple both must have an orgasm, or the even more harmful myth that simultaneous orgasm should be the goal, then the relationship will probably be much poorer because of these beliefs. It is fine to be orgasmic or even orgasmic simultaneously, but to overemphasize the idea that orgasms *must* happen is dangerous because it negates spontaneous responses and puts stringent demands on what should be an enjoyable, free-flowing sexual experience.

What the couple is forgetting about and losing is the sense of sharing and intimacy. The couple which is able to feel comfortable in giving and receiving pleasure and sharing a sense of intimacy in a non-demanding context will be a sexually well-functioning couple. When the couple makes intercourse or orgasm the criterion for their success and measures their roles as lovers and the worth of the experience by this criterion, they lose the sense of sharing and intimacy. A much better viewpoint is that a feeling of mutual sharing and satisfaction is a better criterion for the couple's feelings about the sexual experience. It is important to be aware that every couple can enjoy a non-orgasmic experience, and that a fulfilling intimacy can be shared just by being together. To set a demand on the situation leads to concentrating on the goal and neglecting the main reason one is there — simply to share and enjoy.

The unique aspect of this approach is that with a pleasant, sharing experience you both win; it is not a competition in which one partner wins and one loses.

TOUCHING

One of the best aspects of a relationship is touching. If the touching is pleasant and creates no anxiety in one's partner, it frees both of the partners to remain much closer to their own feelings of warmth and togetherness. In non-demand positions and situations, a couple can feel close and intimate in a stress-free atmosphere. There should be spontaneous, enjoyable touching and body contact without an expectancy or demand that sexual intercourse *must* follow. If one partner or the couple decides to proceed to sexual intercourse, the decision should be spontaneous, cued by an enjoyment of the situation rather than the feeling typified in the following expression: "We've gone this far — we might as well go all the way."

One of the most important things to be aware of is that the non-demanding touching does not have to occur only in the bed or even in the bedroom. In fact, one of the things which keeps a relationship fresh and spontaneous is the willingness to experiment with a variety of situations. Although most people would consider it improper or uncomfortable to engage in affectionate and sexually arousing touching in a public place, it might be easier to be affectionate on a lonely beach, while walking in a wooded area, or in a car parked by a lake. Even more appropriate is the privacy of your own house — using all the rooms, including some unusual places like the rug in front of the fireplace, the big chair in the den, the dining room table, or even the kitchen floor.

Another important variation upon which to experiment is the amount of clothing. When sexual interaction is discussed, many couples immediately think of nudity. Although this is fine and can be enjoyable, it is not the only way. The female appearing wearing only the male's shirt can be quite enticing, as can the male wearing only his pants without shoes or shirt.

Perhaps the most interesting of all variations concerns positioning. Again, there is no right or normal position to be used in non-demand exercises. The position suggestions below as well as previous suggestions are made to facilitate your exploration of non-demand situations and experiences. The concept of non-demanding touching experiences can do much to keep the sense of spontaneity, experimentation, and communication alive in a relationship. The couple who continually enjoy basic human interactions like kissing, holding hands, and hugging each other are a couple who will continue to enjoy their sensual and sexual functioning.

First Set of Exercises For Chapter 11

First sit and discuss your feelings about the use of non-demanding touching and experiences. Be aware of when and how you feel pressure to perform sexually; this is a trap which can serve to take the spontaneity and mutuality out of your sensual and sexual interactions. In these exercises, there will be no demand except your desires and choices. Talk about setting up and refining a communication "signal system" which will tell your partner if you desire to continue on to intercourse or not. This signal system can be verbal, i.e., "I really want to make love," "Let's have intercourse," "I don't want to go on to intercourse; let me just hold you," "I've enjoyed this, but let's stop now" or non-verbal, i.e., massaging the partner's genitals and switching to an intercourse position, using eye contact to say yes or no, moving your partner's hands from your genitals, etc. Also, your partner should have a signal that says "O.K." or "Not tonight — let's do something else instead." A behavioral guideline is that you should not just say no, but rather suggest something else: a backrub, holding each other, using oral sex or any other suitable alternative.

For this first exercise, be in the bedroom and in the nude. Lying on the bed, the female should position herself close behind her partner, with their entire body lengths touching, her chest to his back, with her knees bent inside his. She should have her arms surrounding his body, and thus he can make contact with her arms and can hold hands with her. (See Figure 15) This is a most effective position for just lying together and feeling warmth and closeness. The male is in a more protected and passive position than usual, and he should be aware of his feelings about this, and allow himself to enjoy the feelings of being cared for. In this exercise, it is the female's prerogative to indicate whether or not she wants to carry this contact on to sexual intercourse. She can use any signal system she wants, verbal or non-verbal; the only criterion of the

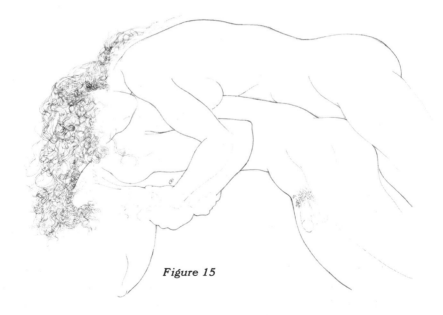

Figure 15

effectiveness of the system is whether her partner clearly receives and understands the communication. If the signal is positive, the male should also be able to signal clearly and directly whether or not he desires to have intercourse. Couples make a mistake in assuming that the male always desires intercourse and they must accede to the female's request for intercourse. To do so sets unrealistic and demanding expectations and pressures. If the male does not desire intercourse, he is advised not simply to say no, but to suggest an alternative positive way to end the experience. One possibility would be just holding his partner. Another might be manually stimulating her to orgasm. Another might be engaging in whole-body touching with both partners' eyes closed, or doing something else which is mutually pleasurable. If the female signals she does not desire intercourse, she should suggest another way to end the experience. One possibility would be to go to sleep in the position shown in Figure 15. Another would be to stimulate her partner orally; another to give a whole-body massage. Either partner should accept the initiative or suggest his or her own; neither should press for intercourse or feel rejected. Remember, the idea is to enjoy a non-demanding sensual and sexual experience.

Second Set of Exercises For Chapter 11

Discuss how the signalling system operated in the last set of exercises. Are you able to feel just as comfortable in initiating intercourse as in just continuing with the pleasuring and ending the experience with no demand for intercourse? Is your partner able to accept your request or to change it to something more enjoyable for him or her? If you decide not to continue to intercourse are there bad feelings, or feelings of pressure or rejection? If there are difficulties, feel free to repeat the first exercise or to use the same roles (female initiate, male respond) with the second set of exercises. If things have gone well, let the male decide whether or not to continue to intercourse this time.

This time choose a place other than the bedroom to interact with each other. It can be the living room, den, basement, or any room you choose. This exercise is best done in the nude so that you can be comfortable with nudity outside the bedroom. Be sure that you won't be disturbed by children. (Being affectionate in front of children is positive for them to see, so that they may be aware that affection and sensuality are a good aspect of people. However, engaging in sexual activity in front of children is sexually healthy neither for the adults nor for the children.)

For these exercises, the male lies on his stomach, arms extended over his head. Even if you are not in bed, you can use throw pillows or pillows from the bedroom. If pillows are being used, his arms can be resting on the pillows. Lying on her side, the female covers his arms, with one hand holding his. Her other arm is free to caress his back, and one leg can be placed over his for even more contact. Ths position allows the female access to touching and caressing her partner's body, and the male can either be passive or can return the caresses. However, since males have the tendency to become overly active and initiating, he should remember that this is a non-demand position where much of the pleasuring and caressing comes from the female. Of course, this position — as all non-demand positions — can be reversed with the male covering, holding, and caressing the female.

In this position, it is the male's prerogative to decide whether or not he wants to carry the contact on to sexual intercourse. He can use a signal system, verbal or non-verbal, to communicate to his partner whether he wants to end the experience on a touching, nondemanding note or to continue to intercourse. The male needs to be expecially attentive to his own feelings and desires, and he also needs to signal for intercourse not because he "should" or is "expected to" but because he really would rather have intercourse than continue with non-demanding touching. Likewise, the female responds with what she really wants to do rather than what she "should" do, not fearing disapproval or repercussions from her partner. Remember, the best way to improve a couple's sexual functioning and communication is to have both partners aware of their feelings and desires and to communicate them clearly and directly to each other. If the desires are different, it is easiest to resolve by doing a positive sensual or sexual activity, rather than one partner simply saying no. You will find that you can communicate and usually can come up with something that is good for both of you.

Third Set of Exercises For Chapter 11

At this point you as a couple are probably aware of the positive aspects of non-demanding touching. You know how it can enhance sexuality and sexual intercourse when you decide to continue to intercourse, and where it can be a positive, affectionate affirmation of you as a couple when you decide not to continue to intercourse. To make non-demand touching more like your real-life sexual functioning, it may be worthwhile to experiment with the amount of clothing you wear and your location somewhere other than the bedroom for this set of exercises.

You might begin the exercise by slowly or teasingly disrobing your partner to a level of undress (other than nudity) in which you find him or her to be the most sexually appealing. Everyone is unique in this respect, and you might test out your feelings. Some females find their partners most enticing when they have only underpants on. Others like them fully clothed on top and nude on the bottom. Do what you like. Some males like their partners best in bra and panties, or with pants and bra hanging, or nude on the bottom with a shirt and a headband; again, your unique tastes are important here.

In continuing the exercise, a male sits propped on pillows comfortably with his legs spread. Facing him, the female lies between his spread legs, with her knees near the side of his body. She also will have pillows behind the lower part of her back so that she is in a good position both to touch and to see her partner. Rather than one partner being primary initiator, this non-demand position allows and encourages both partners to give and receive affection. The couple should be especially aware of using eye contact to facilitate each other's positive feelings about this non-demanding experience. Remember that the most positive aspects of the pleasuring and touching experience are the enjoyment and responsivity.

In the same manner, let the decision whether or not to proceed to intercourse be mutual. Follow your own feelings instead of doing what you think your partner expects. Continue to work toward a clear, honest, and mutual communication system.

Fourth Set of Exercises For Chapter 11

Before beginning, discuss what you have learned from these exercises so far and whether you have fallen into any traps, such as having intercourse every time, not establishing a positive, non-intercourse way of ending an exercise, or one partner always pushing for intercourse. If you have fallen into a trap, discuss what you need to do to work out a really non-demanding aspect of your affectional and sexual relationship. Knowing your trap allows you as a couple to monitor it and not have it continue to affect your relationship negatively.

Approach the last non-demand position with the atmosphere and amount of clothing that you as a couple have decided are most conducive to non-demanding exchanges of affection. Begin the exercise in the male superior position, where the male is lying on top of his partner. The male then moves slowly down his partner's body until his head is resting on the soft stomach area beneath her rib cage. He puts his arms around her body, with her hands being free to caress his head and shoulder area. This position can be particularly arousing because it positions the male where he can easily caress the genital area of the female's body. There is little eye contact, but positionings where there is little eye contact can sometimes be among the most arousing of all. The decision whether to continue with non-demanding touch or to switch to intercourse should be mutual. This experience will provide an opportunity to test your signalling system, since you will not be using eye contact. You can be aware of your own needs and be in tune with your partner's feelings and responses so that the decision simply to enjoy the non-demanding touching or to switch to having sexual intercourse will lead to a smooth transition where both partners feel their needs and desires have been understood and accepted.

AFTERWORD

Feeling comfortable with non-demanding touching and pleasuring is an integral part of a successful sexual relationship. It enhances feelings of affection and sexual interest with the knowledge that not all touching is goal-directed and intercourse-directed. A good guideline to use as a couple is that at least once every two months you reserve an evening for non-demanding touch which does not end in intercourse. This non-demanding touch should also be extended to a variety of non-bedroom situations. To be affectionate with each other is good for your relationship; it provides a positive model for your children. Perhaps the best sex education a child can have is to see his parents hugging, kissing, and demonstrating affection. The message to the child is that you feel good about your bodies, your sensual expression, and yourselves as a couple.

You should also be aware that these non-demand positions are only four of the many that can be used. All can be reversed and can be fun to test out for different feelings when they are reversed. In order to feel more comfortable with non-demand positions and to refine your signal system on whether to proceed to intercourse or not, you will need to continue to be open to experimentation and spontaneity. It is most important to tell your partner your feelings and desires clearly and directly.

12   Sexual Expression for the Aging Couple

One of the biological facts of life is that our bodies are continually changing. These changes are most researched in children and adolescents; much less emphasis and study has been devoted to understanding the aging process. Since bodily changes from aging occur at a slower rate, the changes are much harder to identify and specify.

Your body will be going through or is going through changes that will affect your sexual responses and feelings. Unfortunately, extremely little attention had been given to the effect of aging on sexual functioning until the recent work of Masters and Johnson. Our society tends to be youth-oriented, and it generally ignores adults and, especially, older adults. Also, our society tends to have a rather ambivalent outlook on sexuality generally, and especially sexual expression among older adults. These two trends — ambivalence about aging and adult sexuality — in our society have combined to make the area of sexual expression in aging one of the most myth-ridden and poorly understood areas in human sexuality. Thus, the couple who desire to continue to function comfortably and enjoyably need to be aware of their own bodily changes and changes in their partners. They also need to be able to communicate about these changes and adjust to them.

MYTHS ABOUT AGING

There are many myths about sex and aging which can reasonably be rejected by the couple. A prevalent fallacy is that when a woman reaches menopause her desire for sex naturally ends and any woman who wishes to continue with sex and intercourse is "oversexed." On the contrary, menopause (a topic about which there are many negative myths) simply means that the ability to bear children has ceased. The need for affection and sexual expression continues at the same rate and perhaps an even greater rate, since contraception and fear of impregnation are no longer factors in the lives of post-menopausal women. The male who does not get immediate and strong erections or who feels a lessened need to ejaculate might believe the myth that this means he is "burnt out" sexually. The fact is that taking a longer time to get erections as well as not needing to ejaculate at each sexual opportunity are normal and natural concomitants of the aging process in males. Another myth is that a male has only so many ejaculations, so that if he does not ejaculate that means his sex life is over — he has run out of ejaculations, so he can no longer have intercourse. The reality is that regularity of sexual expression throughout one's life is the best way to promote continued sexual expression as one gets older. Thus, the more sexually active a person has been, the better he is able to function sexually as he ages. It is just not a problem of running out of semen. Another myth is that sex is for the young and beautiful only. As one gets older and lines develop around his eyes, he may be getting too old to be appealing. According to the myth, this means that sexual appeal is gone and therefore so is the need for sexual expression. When people become defensive and self-conscious as they age, they also develop a very self-defeating attitude.

As we age, our needs for warmth, affection, self-esteem, and sexual expression remain high. In fact, continued interest in sensual and sexual functioning is a sign of a good positive psychological and sexual adjustment to aging.

CHANGES DURING AGING

In the aging process there are regular, normal, and predictable changes that take place in the human body, such as wrinkling of the facial skin. The changes that come with aging are generally gradual but defininte; they should be incorporated into the individual's self-image without reduction of self-esteem.

New outlooks on sexual expression must be accepted continually by every person and must be communicated to his partner. However, the couple must be aware that because their bodies might be reacting somewhat differently and somewhat more slowly than they have before, the need for sensual pleasure and sexual expression is still very much there, and it is still a psychologically and sexually healthy need. The sexual responses are simply *different* from what they were previously (different, not worse or poorer). One of a person's basic needs throughout life is the need for a close, warm, loving relationship; with aging this need is often increased rather than lessened. Since life is a balance of physical, social, sexual, and psychological aspects, it makes sense that the social, psychological, and sexual relationships will become more important and involving as the physical state become less intense with aging. From this perspective, our feeling is that sensual and sexual expression can be even more enjoyable and comfortable in the aging couple than in the young or middle-aged couple. Sexual expression can and should be one of the major forces in the life of the aging person and couple.

Although there are definite changes in the male's sexual functioning, it is not as specific and clear as in menopause. The changes in the female body after menopause are rather pronounced. The walls of the vagina usually become smooth and thin, and vaginal lubrication is often much slower and in less volume. The vagina does not expand as rapidly as it once did. If there are distressing or annoying changes, such as painful intercourse or painful spasms in the uterus after orgasm, the woman should consult a gynecologist. She may be experiencing hormonal imbalance. In fact, as a general rule it makes sense to contact a gynecologist regarding sexual expression and the possibility of hormone replacement therapy during and after menopause. It is crucial to tell the gynecologist that continued normal, healthy, sexual expression is important to you. Unfortunately, too many physicians believe the same myths as the lay public about sexual expression for the aging female and couple.

In exchanging information and feelings with your partner, emphasize the gains you have experienced as well as the losses, if any. Changes in response time means that you can spend more time in sensual pleasuring and foreplay activities and that you can enjoy the gradually-building sense of excitement and arousal. Slower response time allows you to spend more time together as an affectionate and loving couple; it also encourages a variety of foreplay and pleasuring experiences.

The following exercises are oriented toward making each individual and you as a couple more comfortable with the changes in your body so that you might continue to share and communicate as a couple. The two major guidelines are first to support your partner as he or she strives to make positive adjustments to the sensual and sexual responses of his or her body, and second to request and guide your partner clearly and directly in exploring new modes of sexual expression that are not always oriented toward the goals of intercourse and orgasm. We hope that the couple has previously read and experienced the self-exploration enhancement exercises, the non-genital touching and pleasuring exercises, the genital touching and pleasuring exercises, and any other exercises that they as a couple wanted to explore.

First Set of Exercises For Chapter 12

First sit and discuss with your partner what is probably the major change in sexual response as a function of aging: the increase in length of time needed for sexual arousal. For the male, an erection which was once gained almost immediately now takes longer to achieve. Also, often the erection is not completely "hard." The female will also be aware of a lessening in vaginal lubrication and an increase in time before feeling is aroused.

Begin the exercise by taking a relaxing, sensuous bath or shower together. Afterwards, simply lie together in bed, seeing each other and being aware of your partner's body and feeling close together. Begin to make physical contact with each other, in a sensuous, warm, non-demanding manner. Intermix the non-genital and genital touching from the beginning and be aware of your own and your partner's gradually growing arousal. Accept it rather than trying to force it or speed it up. Rather than reaching into the vagina to spread the lubrication around the vulval area, the male can gently massage around the mons, the clitoris, and the labial area. Do not focus attention on the vagina until your partner is showing signs of arousal.

The female can appreciate and enjoy massaging and caressing her partner's penis and genital area, and be accepting of the erection slowly building (although not necessarily getting completely firm). Enjoy your ability to increase your partner's arousal slowly and comfortably. Throughout be non-demanding and notice the relaxed, sensuous atmosphere and how it compares favorably to the performance-demanding, goal-oriented atmosphere you might have felt in your youth. When you both feel aroused, you can decide to proceed to intercourse or you can decide just to stay with this good feeling. If you choose the latter, while experiencing it, discuss your reactions and feelings to the lengthening of arousal time. If you decide to go on to intercourse, be sure to set aside some time later to sit and talk over a drink, or coffee, or a snack and discuss your feelings about your own body changes and those of your partner. Check out whether there are any things not understood or any misconceptions. How do you feel about the less firm erection? Do you miss the heavier flow of vaginal lubrication? Do you understand your partner's gradual arousal cycle? Integrate these changes into your feelings about you as a sexual person and yourselves as an affectionate and sexual couple.

Second Set of Exercises For Chapter 12

Now that you have a better sense of the enjoyment of pleasuring foreplay and you understand how the lengthened time for sexual arousal can add to the sexual experience, it is time to focus on the changes in the intercourse experience itself. The major changes for the female are that her vaginal walls are thinner and less flexible; the vaginal lubrication is decreased; and the intensity of the orgasmic response is somewhat diminished. For the male, he no longer feels the demand to have an orgasm at each intercourse opportunity; the amount of semen ejaculated is decreased in volume; the ejaculation is less intense; and it is easier to maintain ejaculatory control. Also, ejaculation occurs over a longer process with one stage rather than two sharply-defined stages. Following ejaculation, the resolution stage is shorter, and the erection is lost more rapidly after ejaculation.

The couple should first discuss their understanding of these changes in their own body and responses, and then discuss questions they have about the responses of their partner. They should make the discussion frank, explicit, and honest. The female might want to ask her partner how he feels about her vaginal containment and how he feels about the way she responds orgasmically now as compared to twenty years ago. The male might want to discuss his partner's reaction when he does not ejaculate, or ask if she can still feel his semen in her vagina, or how she feels about his erection rapidly decreasing.

Remember, it is important to understand natural bodily changes, to support your partner in making positive adjustments to them, and to support each other in continuing to use intercourse as a positive experience of sexual expression. Be open to the positive and enjoyable experiences that are now more available to you as a result of the aging process — specifically the male's ability to control ejaculation better and the female's better understanding of her vaginal feelings and sensations as well as your mutual awareness of gradual, non-demanding whole-body sensual and sexual arousal.

Begin the exercise by using what you have learned and shared with each other about the extended and gradual foreplay and pleasuring process. Use the pleasuring techniques — non-genital touching, genital touching, oral stimulation, whole body contact, non-demand positions, etc. — that are most effective for you. Enjoy the gradual build-up of sexual arousal, and take pleasure in observing the excitement and arousal of your partner. Be supportive, warm, and loving. This adds to your sensual and sexual responsivity.

Instead of demanding that her partner get an erection (such a demand simply increases pressure, which increases male anxiety and in turn decreases the firmness of the erection), the woman can use various techniques of manual or oral penile stimulation and see that as the arousal builds so will the erection. Likewise, the male can deal sensitively with the lack of lubrication, accepting and supporting the fact that his partner may be responding emotionally but that her physiological responses are more extended. He should not raise her anxiety about this, because that would decrease lubrication, but rather continue with the sensually and sexually arousing activities which naturally lead to heightened arousal and lubrication.

In initiating intercourse, be sure that both of you are really ready to begin. Do not pressure or push yourself or your partner. Be sure there is good vaginal lubrication. Even if the male's erection is not completely firm and hard, be satisfied he is aroused and it is firm enough to ensure easy penetration. Allow the female to guide intromission. She should do it gradually so that there is no discomfort at the vaginal opening or in the vagina itself. She can guide the penis and direct penile thrusting so that it gives her the maximum feeling of sensation and enjoyment. During the intercourse itself, rather than pushing for quick sexual release, continue slow, tender, and rhythmic movements and enjoy the warmth and growing arousal. Instead of focusing solely on penis-vagina contact, feel free to touch and caress each other's entire body. One of the real advantages of non-rushed, non-demanding intercourse experience is that you can enjoy the entire body experience and not fall into the youthful trap of expecting and demanding rapid genital release. In terms of the orgasm experience, the woman should enjoy her feelings and notice that it is more a whole-body sensation rather than an intense sensation focused only in the pelvic are. As the male ejaculates, he can also focus on the whole-body feeling which has been developed throughout foreplay and pleasuring and intercourse. Thus, for both the man and woman the key is to emphasize the gains and sensations of sexual and sensual feelings throughout their bodies, while accepting the less intense feelings of sexual release in their genital areas.

To complete the sexual experience, you can bask in the afterplay or afterglow period. While holding and touching each other, talk about how you can continue the intercourse experience as a vital part of your life and your relationship.

Third Set of Exercises For Chapter 12

This set of exercises focuses on making a positive adjustment to one of the more threatening aspects of the aging process — the lessened need of the male for ejaculation. Throughout their sexual lives, most males ejaculate at almost every intercourse experience. In youth, if the male is too fatigued, has drunk too much, or is otherwise physically below par, he might not ejaculate during intercourse. He often considers failure to ejaculate a negative experience. Thus the male does not have the appropriate experience or expectation to understand and cope with a change in ejaculatory demand. On the other hand, the sexually functional female understands a lessened need for orgasmic response from her own experiences. Typically, the sexually functional female is not orgasmic at each sexual opportunity. Rather, she enjoys the orgasmic experiences, but also learns to enjoy and accept the non-orgasmic experiences and not consider them as negative. In fact, many women find that they enjoy certain aspects of the non-orgasmic experience more than the orgasmic experiences. But she may be used to her partner's having an ejaculation each time, and she will often overreact negatively when he does not ejaculate. The female can and should support her partner's making a positive adjustment to his altered ejaculatory demand.

What the male must understand and accept is that as he grows older the need to ejaculate decreases. While the erection may be strong, and arousal complete and full, the male can have intercourse pleasurably but perhaps without ejaculation at each opportunity. Essentially the male must make the kind of change of attitude and approach which his partner has had for the past thirty years. He must realize that being sensual, sexual, and affectionate is most important, and that ejaculatory response will exist when the flesh is able, but that the absence is not indicative of a lack of interest or pleasure on the part of the male.

This exercise should be done a day or two after an ejaculatory experience and where the male is now feeling little to no ejaculatory demand. The idea is for both partners to experience the sexual interchange and the intercourse experience as an enjoyable and positive one where the male will not have an ejaculation. In the foreplay and pleasuring both partners should focus on making the sexual interaction very arousing and enjoyable, prolonging it and enjoying it. At intromission, be aware that even though there will not be an ejaculation, the penis is still quite erect and the pleasure of intromission is still very much present. During intercourse itself the male can at first focus on the enjoyment of his partner. If she is aroused and desirous of orgasm they should participate together to help her be orgasmic and both enjoy the experience of her sexual satisfaction. Because the male is now aware that at this intercourse opportunity he does not have the demand or desire to ejaculate, he can experiment with several different alternatives to continuing this sexual experience and making it positive. He might just want to continue thrusting, or he might try a different movement or rhythm of thrusting. He might want to cease intercourse and go back to being manually stimulated; he may want to request his partner to use oral-genital stimulation, or just roll over and hold his partner, or lie back and allow his partner to give him a whole-body massage using lotion or oil, or maybe just sit and talk while affectionately touching, or anything which would feel sensuous and enjoyable for him. The idea is to make this a sensual, sexually positive experience where the couple learn that they can enjoy an intercourse experience which does not end in ejaculation. The trap for the male is to feel that he has lost something if he does not ejaculate — and therefore to push himself to ejaculate. The trap for the female is to commiserate with her partner about his "failure." These traps are very self-defeating and defeating for you as a sexually expressive couple. In the same way that a female can have a positive sensual and sexual experience without orgasm, so can the male. In fact, the male (and you as a couple) should find that sensual techniques can make this non-ejaculatory experience a quite enjoyable one.

Your sexual experience as a couple will be greatly enhanced if you both feel positive about non-ejaculatory intercourse experiences. Ejaculating only when there is ejaculatory demand, and accepting this as normal, will do much to maintain enjoyment of intercourse into your seventies and eighties, and even longer.

After the intercourse experience, give each other feedback concerning your feelings about non-ejaculatory intercourse. Discuss how you can continue to make this a positive part of your sexual relationship, and how you can increase your enjoyment of the experience. Feel free to experiment with other techniques of enjoying the non-ejaculation intercourse experience.

Fourth Set of Exercises For Chapter 12

For the last exercise, set aside a relatively long free period of time (perhaps three hours or more). Decide you are going to make this a very special experience. You may want to include a bottle of your favorite wine, or mixed drink, or favorite exotic tea. You might want to put on your favorite records or read your favorite poems or look at your favorite pictures.

Begin by taking a sensuous, warm bath or shower. Then lie in bed nude. The male should begin by caressing his partner's body, and while caressing describe it to her as it is now and how it has changed over the years. If at any point the female feels uncomfortable, she can interrupt him and discuss what he said or is feeling. The woman should feel and be aware of her body and listen carefully to her partner's comments and his feelings. Do not focus on feelings of what you have lost, but rather on here-and-now impressions and feelings about your body. Trust your partner's perceptions and feelings; listen to what he says about the lovely and attractive parts of your body. Be aware of and accept your bodily changes. There is more to your relationship and your body sensations than the young firm breast that now is heavier. It is still your breast and still a part of you. If you accept your bodily changes gracefully, you will find it easier to be a sensual and graceful aging woman.

The male should continue to be supportive and loving with his partner, both verbally and by touch. Many times just the fact that she knows her partner has noticed the changes and is still warm and loving can do nice things for a relationship.

Then switch roles, and let the woman caress her partner's body while being aware of and verbally commenting on the bodily changes she's noticed over the years. In noticing and discussing all of the body changes, be loving and supportive. Be open and honest with each other in acknowledging the changes and differences in bodily responses, while continuing to show understanding, support and affection. The male should be aware of his body; he should note the differences in capacity of responses, and he should try to get a greater awareness of the positive sensations of prolonged touching and sensual feelings. Rather than the aging process taking away his sexual expression, it is building and reinforcing sensual, affectionate, and whole-body feelings.

Allow yourselves to come together in a sexually arousing manner. Your intercourse experience during this time can follow an extended period of foreplay and mutual enjoyment of each other's bodies. After the sexual encounter, stay with your feelings of closeness and mutual sharing. Enjoy the afterplay or afterglow experience and allow yourself then to continue to arouse each other. As you do so notice the time needed by the male to begin getting an erection and the decreased need for a second ejaculatory experience. Notice that once an erection is achieved it is usually easy to maintain. The female should be aware that her need for sexual release is less strong but that her need for touching and affection remain strong. Allow your second coming together to be a sensuous, whole-body experience that will do away with any past fears or negative feelings about your attractiveness and sexual expression. The sexual coming together should not culminate in intercourse unless you both desire it to, but it should lead to good feelings about you and your sexuality.

You have set aside the time, so use it to talk with each other about your understanding and acceptance of your own and your partner's changing with aging. You owe it to yourself as well as to you both as a couple to enjoy your older years, the feelings of caring, affection, sensual feelings, and sexual expression.

AFTERWORD

The aging years constitute one of the most significant times in every person's life for feelings of affection, total enjoyment of sensuality, and effective sexual expression. Sexuality in older persons is perfectly normal. The best way to ensure effective sexual functioning as you grow older is to stay actively involved in sensual and sexual touching and activity, but not to make demands to perform sexually each time. In essence, you need to enjoy and appreciate your own body, your partner's body, and the sensual and sexual contact. They continue to be an important part of your relationship. This is the best way to ensure positive sexual functioning into your seventies and eighties.

13 Increasing Comfort with Sexual Intercourse

Throughout these exercises, we have emphasized non-goal orientation, feeling comfortable with giving and receiving pleasure, and being aware of and responsive to both sensual and sexual stimulation. These basic guidelines for increasing awareness and comfort also apply to intercourse. All too often couples consider pleasuring and foreplay as important only to get in the mood. They seem to think that intercourse is the "real thing." Our view is that pleasuring and foreplay, intercourse, and afterglow are part of a continuous, flowing process. Intercourse, then, is not an isolated sexual activity.

INTERACTION
If the pleasuring and foreplay are slow, tender, rhythmic, and natural, they will set the tone for a natural progression into intercourse which is mutually satisfying. Rather than being simply a mechanical process of juxtaposing two bodies, sexual intercourse involves the interaction of needs, feelings, and mutual pleasure for a couple. A popular myth is that foreplay is for the female to enjoy,

but intercourse is primarily for the male's sexual satisfaction and he must always or nearly always initiate it. From other exercises you should be aware that both of you can enjoy the pleasuring and foreplay, and it is not only acceptable but preferable that both partners feel free to initiate intercourse. The female often enjoys and gains as much (and sometimes more) from the intercourse experience as the male. Furthermore, rather than the female being the passive recipient of intercourse, it is important that she feel free to initiate and actively participate. By its very nature, sexual intercourse implies mutuality, reciprocity, and sharing. Equally important, sexual intercourse is most likely to be most enjoyable if each person is attuned to the needs, feelings, and preferences of his or her partner, as well as his own responses. Intercourse can be thought of as the natural culmination of a positive, intense experience of sexual sharing which usually begins with communication (both verbal and non-verbal) between the couple, moves to holding, kissing, and caressing, then into the pleasuring and foreplay, into intercourse, and finally to the afterglow.

INTERCOURSE TRAPS

The three main traps couples fall into regarding intercourse are:

1. To separate psychologically the interaction and foreplay and pleasuring from intercourse.
2. To make the act of intercourse *per se* a mechanical or stereotypical response.
3. To make intercourse simply a matter of emotionless penile-vaginal interactions.

To be aware of these traps so that you might monitor yourself, the major thing to keep in mind is the give-to-get principle. The best way to insure a positive mutual experience is to give pleasure to your partner, so that he or she might be aroused and responsive to you, which in turn can cause greater feelings of sexual arousal.

Some couples put major emphasis on both partners having orgasm during intercourse. Although orgasmic response is obviously important and desirable, to make it an absolute goal is a mistake. A much better attitude seems to be to consider orgasm during intercourse as desirable only when both partners want it and to realize that non-orgasmic intercourse can be a positive experience for you as a couple. Two things are very important to keep in mind regarding the relationship between intercourse and orgasm. First, the female sexual response is much more complex than the male's. She might be non-orgasmic, orgasmic, or multi-orgasmic. If your attitude as a couple demands that the female be orgasmic during each intercourse experience, you are not accepting the reality of female sexuality; you inhibit the female, as well as yourselves as a couple, from full sexual expression. The second important factor is that there are non-intercourse methods of orgasm, especially foreplay, afterglow, and oral-genital stimulation. These are all normal and important sexual expressions which couples should feel free to utilize either in conjunction with intercourse or on some occasions rather than intercourse.

AFTERGLOW INTERACTION

Whether or not intercourse results in orgasm for you as a couple, the afterglow interactions are extremely important. Quite frequently, couples see orgasm as a goal and once this goal is reached, they feel that the sexual encounter is over. This is a myth, both from a physiological and psychological viewpoint. Masters and Johnson isolated four phases of sexual response: excitement, plateau, orgasmic, and resolution. Thus, from a strictly physiological point of view, an afterglow experience is important, since it corresponds to the body's return to a less intense state. From the psychological viewpoint an even stronger case can be made for the importance of afterglow. You have just shared a meaningful physical and emotional experience. Afterglow is a means of showing your partner that you enjoyed him or her, that it was a good physical and orgasmic experience — good for you as a couple. The pleasuring starts as a sensual experience and the afterglow ends the sexual interaction as a sensual experience; the afterglow is just as important to a growing sexual relationship as foreplay and pleasuring are.

NOVELTY

One means of establishing and maintaining satisfying sexual intercourse is for you as a couple to be experimental, spontaneous, and innovative. All too often couples assume that there is only one proper way for them to engage in intercourse — that is, with the male above, face-to-face with the woman (this is the male-superior position which is described in detail later). Within our culture, this is by far the preferred and most commonly employed intercourse position. However, it is a myth that male superior is the only normal or right position. Intercourse position is strictly a matter of the couple's desires and preferences. As long as you and your partner are comfortable with and positive toward them, exploring the variety of intercourse positions does not involve your acquiring new skills or becoming acrobats or contortionists. Rather, exploration and experimentation mean acquiring a basic knowledge about the major varieties of intercourse positions, and simultaneously being aware of your own and your partner's needs, feelings, and preferences.

We feel that without exploration and experimentation you as a couple run the risk of developing rather stereotyped intercourse experiences, which might then become dull and unrewarding. Once sexual experiences become routine, they also tend to become rather mechanical and chore-like rather than a sharing experience for the couple. In fact, although we have emphasized slow, tender, gentle, rhythmic touching and intercourse, if each of your intercourse experiences were this way they would become boring and dull.

We do not want to fall into the trap of so many marriage and sex manuals of writing a "cookbook" describing in great detail an endless variety of intercourse positions and postures. In such manuals, the message to the couple is that to be a good lover you have to prove yourself a masterful technician. When sexual intercourse becomes a gymnastic experience and feat, it also becomes a detached, impersonal, and unfeeling kind of interaction. Rather, our message regarding variation and exploration in intercourse is that choices are open to all couples who are interested in continuing to grow and share their sexual experiences. Spontaneity and experimentation refer to being aware of your own needs and desires, and feeling free to express them.

Your experimentation and variation in approach are based on what you have learned about yourself and each other, and depend on your sharing, giving feedback, and feeling comfortable. To reemphasize a point made earlier, sexual intercourse is a form of psychological sharing and mutuality which takes into account the needs, feelings and preferences of two people. With this prime consideration in mind, it is our feeling that you as a couple can expand your sexual awareness through exploring a number of intercourse positions.

POSITION VARIATIONS

Popular misconceptions suggest that sexual intercourse has no limits with regard to positions; in reality the basic intercourse positions are few in number. We shall be outlining the four basic positions, although you should be aware that there are many variations on these basic themes as well as several other positions. Our feeling is that sexual interactions should not be used for either partner to prove something (sexual prowess, physical agility, or the ability to do it better than in the book). Rather, the intercourse positions and variations can be realized best by you as a couple developing your own unique styles — styles which are comfortable, enjoyable, and fun for you.

To use the analogy of ice cream shops to discuss variations in intercourse positions, some people like to try only vanilla; others try to or three flavors that seem really attractive; others try nine or ten and then stay with one or two but once a month try an exotic one; and still others try all and want a different one each time. This is simply an example of individual differences in preferences. It is not a question of what is normal or abnormal, but simply a matter of difference in styles. The couple should discuss their preferences and feel free to follow them in intercourse positions.

The exercises on intercourse positions are the last set of exercises in this series. Throughout the exercises we have emphasized the importance of a non-demand and non-goal orientation. The reason for this, we feel, is that the role of intercourse and orgasm has been overemphasized to the detriment of naturally developing sensual and sexual responses. Our approach to intercourse is that it follows the same principles of slowness, tender and gentle touching, and natural and rhythmic movement you have learned previously. Intercourse should simply be a smooth transition from the pleasuring and foreplay experience. Getting responses from your partner is important, and making known your own feelings is important. Obviously, intercourse will be a typical outcome of the ordinary pleasuring and foreplay experience. However, we advise couples that a good guideline is to do pleasuring which does not end in intercourse once a month or once every other month or whenever they feel a need to be intimate with their partners but do not desire intercourse. (It is easy to fall back into the trap of all touching being intercourse-oriented and to lose appreciation of the touching and pleasuring process *per se*.) In this way you continue to build your appreciation for non-genital and genital pleasuring and your awareness of sensuality. An added benefit is that the intercourse experience can be enhanced when it occurs as a choice rather than as an each-and-every-time experience.

First Set of Exercises For Chapter 13

Before beginning, sit and talk about what you as an individual and you as a couple have learned in the non-genital touching, genital touching and pleasuring, and other non-demand exercises you have experienced. Share with each other your feelings in particular about the non-goal oriented experiences you have had. You might talk about ways you as a couple can monitor yourselves so that you stop falling into the trap of making intercourse a pressured, goal-oriented task.

Then discuss your previous experience, if any, with the female superior position. Especially discuss your feelings about the common myth that the male should always be the aggressor and dominant figure in sexual interaction and the female should always be the passive partner. The reason this position is presented first is that for some sexual difficulties using the female superior position is recommended (i.e., problems of non-orgasmic response and ejaculatory control), but even more importantly it allows the couple to experiment with a position that encourages the female to be more active and initiatory. At first glance, the female superior position may seem threatening for both males and females. However, in reality, it neither threatens nor impinges upon feelings of femininity or masculinity. Rather, it allows a mutually enhancing variation in sexual expression. It facilitates the female's being more sexually expressive and active, which enhances her feelings about her own sexuality. It allows the male to experience his partner's activity (which often can be sexually arousing), but even more important, it allows the male to enjoy the feeling of receiving pleasure rather than always having to be the aggressive initiator. This is very likely to expand the male's feelings and awareness, and to enhance his feelings about his masculinity and sexuality.

Once you've talked these things out and have understood your partner's feelings, proceed with the experience. Start by getting back into the same comfortable experiences you had during the non-genital touching. At first, let the pleasuring and foreplay be based on one partner as pleasurer and the other as pleasuree. Slowly allow the transition to a more mutual and natural pleasuring, feeling comfortable in utilizing manual and oral techniques you have experienced previously. Allow the movement to be slow, tender, gentle, natural, and rhythmic, and make the transition to intercourse unhurried and flowing. The male should be lying comfortably on the bed, with the female straddling him on his upper thigh region, with her knees bent and resting comfortably on the bed.

Once you are comfortable in this position don't immediately initiate intercourse. Rather, continue with the pleasuring, allowing the sense of arousal and excitement to build. Even though the male is in the more passive position, he can still feel free to touch and stroke his partner actively, including manually stimulating the vulval area or running his penis around her mons and clitoral area. In experimenting with this position, the female should be the one to initiate intromission when both she and her partner feel aroused. One of the advantages of this position is that the female can guide the movement, the contact of the penis with the vaginal opening, and the extent of penile penetration as well. In guiding intromission, the female gently and unhurriedly inserts her

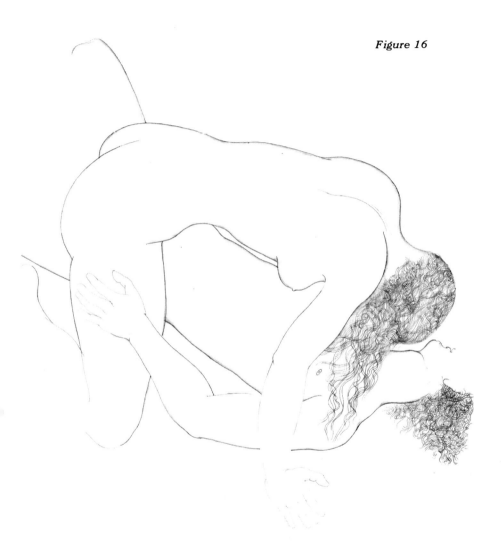

Figure 16

partner's penis into her vagina. Rather than sitting back, she should insert it by sliding back at a forty-five degree angle. Also, in experimenting with this position and giving the female more freedom of activity, she can both initiate and direct the point of vaginal-penile contact, and utilize what she's learned from previous exercises about increasing vaginal feeling and arousal. She can also feel free to utilize the type of thrusting involving rapid up and down movement, thrusting involving a rhythmic, circular movement, or any variation or combination which she finds arousing. Her partner should also be aware of what kinds of thrusting and penile movement are comfortable and arousing for him. Experimenting and giving feedback are the best ways to establish mutually enjoyable intercourse. (See Figure 16)

During intercourse, the male can utilize his greater freedom to caress, stroke, and fondle his partner's body sensually. He can also stimulate her clitoris manually, which might facilitate orgasmic response. Another advantage the male should be aware of and enjoy is that ejaculatory control is considerably easier in female-superior than other positions. He can enjoy the freedom of ejaculatory control, and the prolongation of sensual and sexual enjoyment for both. Also, both partners can be aware of and utilize the feeling cues from facial expressions which are easily observed in the female superior position. Generally, this is an excellent position for both non-verbal and verbal communication, and the couple can make the most of this opportunity.

One of the most cited disadvantages of this intercourse position is that because the male is not in control of the coital thrusting, his penis could lose containment in the vagina and slip out. Something you might want to experiment with is the actual loss of penile containment. Rather than reacting with anxiety or even panic (this is especially true of the male), simply use this break in intercourse to do some pleasuring and then later proceed with a second intromission. Losing penile containment does not have to be a negative experience or an event to be feared. Rather than trying to reinsert the penis immediately, you can enjoy an added period of manual or oral sensual and sexual pleasuring, and when you both feel aroused and desirous of coming together again in intercourse, return to the position you first used (in this case the female superior) and allow the reentry to be natural and comfortable. Loss of containment occasionally is to be expected. The reason so many couples exclusively use the male superior position is that it is the easiest position for intromission and it is easier to maintain penile-vaginal containment. However, staying with the male superior position just to gain this sense of security inhibits sexual expression.

Many couples have a difficult time in the transition from the end of intercourse to the initiation of afterglow or afterplay. Moving from intercourse to afterglow should be a comfortable, flowing transition rather than an abrupt stop followed by beginning something else. For many couples, intercourse ends when the male has an orgasm and, for others, when both partners have an orgasm. What you as a couple can be aware of and accept is that the achievement of orgasm at each intercourse is a poor criterion for sexual satisfaction. Generally, at each intercourse opportunity the male will have an orgasm. However, this is not always true, specifically among older males. Sometimes, the female will be non-orgasmic; sometimes singly orgasmic; and sometimes multi-orgasmic. Remember, the female sexual response is more complex than the male sexual response. The female might have an orgasmic experience in foreplay or she might not desire an orgasmic experience in that sexual encounter.

When the male pressures his partner to be orgasmic, both people will feel very demanded-upon and frustrated as a consequence. Thus, achievement of orgasm is not a particularly good way to determine when intercourse has ended. Perhaps the best way of looking at it is that there is no clear demarcation between intercourse and afterglow or afterplay.

However, in this exercise, allow the intercourse activity to continue at least until the male has had an orgasm. At that point the female might not feel the need to have an orgasm, or she might have already had an orgasm or had several orgasms. If this is true, simply decrease the amount of sexual movement, stay in the female superior intercourse position for at least a minute, hold and touch each other, and give feedback on the feelings you have after intercourse. Then switch positions to a comfortable, afterglow position where you can see and touch each other. You may want to have tissue or a towel near so that you can wipe off the semen, or, if you are comfortable with the feel of the semen on your body, you might decide not to wash it away. Once you are in a comfortable position, be aware of both your own and your partner's resolution, or "coming down," reactions. Share how you feel and also what you would like your partner to do — be playful, hold you, play with your hair, rub your chest, etc. Be aware of the afterflow and afterplay as a good and comfortable time. Sometimes couples become re-aroused during this time, and decide to proceed with further pleasuring or intercourse. If this happens, that is fine. However, don't push yourselves (especially the male) to this end. Remember that second erections are usually less easy to attain for the male and second orgasms are sometimes less fulfilling. Generally, afterflow or afterplay should simply be a positive sharing experience, not oriented toward re-arousal.

In situations where the female desires an additional or first orgasmic experience after the male has had his orgasm, it is important that she clearly make this known to her partner. The male should *never* insist that *she* push herself to have an orgasm. This is one of the few absolutes we believe in, since we've seen the negative results of this pressure in many couples. If she does desire an orgasm, the male can decide to continue with intercourse. Usually, males partially lose their erections after ejaculation, and continued intercourse movement is sometimes irritating to the penis. Continue intercourse only if it is comfortable for the male. Otherwise, there are several techniques that can be utilized to bring orgasmic return for the woman. One is to use manual vaginal stimulation, possibly including vaginal insertion, at the same time orally stimulating the breasts. Another is to use cunnilingus (oral stimulation of the vulval area). A third is to stimulate manually around the clitoral area. There are also obvious combinations and variations of these techniques as well as other stimulation techniques you have previously utilized to being orgasmic return. After orgasm occurs, the couple can continue holding and touching in the afterglow phase. Even if, and sometimes especially if, there is no orgasm for one or both partners, the afterglow experience is important. Instead of ending with a sense of unfulfillment or frustration, the afterglow interaction allows a positive end to the sexual experience.

Of course, it is quite natural and normal that some sexual experiences will be mediocre and at least a few will be downright uneventful. It is important to accept this fact, and not to exert pressure to make each experience great or memorable. In fact, being able to accept and even to laugh about a not-so-great sexual experience is quite important for a couple.

Obviously, there are many changes and variations that you can utilize with the female superior position and many variations of afterglow. This is true of other intercourse positions we will be talking about, and many of the things we mention to try out in this intercourse position are equally applicable to other intercourse positions. After this exercise, sit and share feelings about it; discuss what you liked and didn't like about it; discuss what things you need to refine so that you can utilize this position more comfortably. Remember, the first try at anything (recall your first experience with non-genital touching) is important mostly in terms of experimentation. It takes practice and feedback in order to feel really comfortable with intercourse and afterglow techniques.

Second Set of Exercises For Chapter 13

The male superior has been by far the most popular intercourse position among American couples. If you are a couple who use it most often or even exclusively, discuss what aspects of the position are particularly enjoyable to you. Some of the commonly mentioned advantages of the male superior position are that it allows you face-to-face interaction which makes communication (verbal and non-verbal) easy and permits kissing, which many couples find highly enjoyable. Penile intromission is easiest in this position and penile containment is relatively easy to maintain. The male can control the thrusting and rhythm and it allows some opportunity for sustained penile penetration after the male ejaculates. It also allows deeper vaginal penetration. Discuss whether you as a couple use these to advantage when you utilize the male superior position. If you are not using the male superior position to the advantage you'd like, discuss how you might use these exercises to learn and experiment to make it more mutually enjoyable and comfortable.

In beginning this series of exercises, what you might do is spend more than your usual amount of time in pleasuring and foreplay. In doing so, utilize some of the more uncommon or esoteric pleasuring techniques that you have learned from previous pleasuring exercises or perhaps ones that you have developed uniquely for yourselves. Thus, although this exercise will be using the most common intercourse position, you can hold to the feeling of experimentation by utilizing a variety of pleasuring experiences.

As a couple, continue the pleasuring experience until the female signals or initiates movement toward intercourse. Both partners should enjoy the pleasuring and allow the arousal to build before actually beginning intercourse. Although at times small amounts of foreplay and quick and vigorous intercourse can be very enjoyable, one of the biggest mistakes couples make is to begin intercourse before they, but especially the female, feel aroused enough to begin.

The female should be sure she's comfortable. She might rest comfortably on her back with legs apart and knees slightly bent. Or she can elevate her pelvis by putting a pillow under her buttocks. The male can partially support himself by having his knees and elbows placed comfortably on the pillow or bed. Generally, he should avoid making his partner uncomfortable by requiring her to support his full body weight. When he removes some of his body weight from her, the couple is somewhat freer to control the extent and rhythm of pelvic movement mutually, although in this exercise the male will essentially control the thrusting. (See Figure 17) Once you are comfortable in the male superior position, do not immediately proceed to intromission. Instead, enjoy foreplay where the male runs his penis around his partner's vulval and clitoral area. The female should focus on the feelings of pleasure that the sensations of the penis give her. During this exercise, the female should take the initiative in guiding him into her vagina. The male can then take the initiative and begin the coital thrusting in a slow, steady, rhythmic movement. He might try penetration not deeper than one and one-half inches into the vagina (roughly two finger joints), keeping the thrusting motions very slow and rhythmic. He should be aware of his partner's reactions and feedback. Even if she becomes quite excited, he should not abruptly make the thrusting more rapid but rather slowly increase the

Figure 17

rhythm. Notice both your own and your partner's reaction to slow, rhythmic and steady thrusting.

Generally, the male enjoys the feeling of ejaculation a great deal. When the male ejaculates he should be aware of, and, in fact, increase the positive sensations of the ejaculation by then thrusting more deeply into the vagina. The female should be aware of her partner's excitement during ejaculation and her own feelings as he ejaculates. If she can focus on her awareness of the ejaculation and the feeling of the semen in her vagina, this focusing can enhance her own enjoyment.

After the ejaculation, stay together in this position for a minute or so, look at your partner and communicate to him or her your feelings about the intercourse experience that you have just shared. In the afterglow experience you might want to do something to make it playful rather than comfortable or intimate. You might want to have a pillow fight, tickle each other, do a frivolous game with your hands or fingers, or anything you have developed as a couple which is a way to express your playful feelings with each other.

In terms of other experiences with the male superior position, be aware of the many variations of the position, including having the woman's legs fully elevated and resting on the male's shoulders; putting a pillow under the woman's buttocks to adjust the vaginal placement against her partner's penis; having the woman lock her legs around her partner's body, and other variations which fit your unique style as a couple. Remember that this position is the most common because it has advantages for both the male and female. Feel free to experiment with variations in pleasuring and foreplay, intercourse, and afterglow so that you as a couple might more fully experience and enjoy the male superior position.

Third Set of Exercises For Chapter 13

Before beginning this set of exercises, discuss what you have learned about your styles of working together and experimenting. The lateral side-by-side coital position has been viewed by many as the most enjoyable and arousing of the intercourse positions. However, this position does not come naturally. Rather, it takes a good deal of working together and communicating from the couple, as well as tolerating some unsuccessful early tries.

There are many variations of the lateral position. In this exercise we focus on one variation: the "scissors" position. Before beginning, agree with your partner that you will use this exercise to explore and experiment and not become frustrated with yourself or your partner if it does not work immediately. To feel comfortable in the lateral coital position, a single attempt will probably not afford the necessary opportunity for all its benefits to be experienced.

You might want to begin by engaging in mutual pleasuring so you can enjoy the experience of both giving and receiving pleasure simultaneously. Feel free to move around and change the pleasuring positions. You will notice that some changes are smooth transitions (i.e., from the male stimulating the woman's breast to the couple mutually kissing and holding each other) while other changes punctuate the rhythm of the pleasuring (i.e., after holding each other side by side, the woman disengaging and moving behind him on her knees to massage her partner's forehead). Be aware of your reaction to smooth transitions as opposed to more abrupt changes. Both are good and add to the variety of the sexual experience; however, in most sexual interchanges many couples prefer more smooth transitions.

The easiest manner in which to get into the lateral coital position is from the female superior position. The reason is that penile intromission is difficult from the lateral coital position.

From the female superior position, the female, kneeling, moves slightly forward on the male's chest. As she moves forward, the male helps her place her extended leg behind her. She raises her other leg in a bent-knee fashion over the male's upper thigh (approaching his waist level). On the side where the female has her leg extended toward the foot of the bed, the male's other leg is extended parallel to the female's extended leg. Before proceeding they should be comfortable and set in this position. The female then puts her head by her partner's shoulder. (See Figure 18) They can roll gently and comfortably to a side-by-side position. We sould suggest that the first time you try this you do not have the penis inserted in the vagina. The reason is that in the rolling, the penis sometimes slips out. To prevent this, when the couple rolls, the male should hold the woman's buttocks so that the penile-vaginal connection is more secure.

Figure 18

If while getting into the position, or during intercourse itself, you do lose penile connection, do not become upset. Simply return to the female superior position, and use the transition to touch and pleasure your partner. Do not immediately attempt reinsertion, but rather make yourselves comfortable and pleasure and fondle your partner in a way you could not while you were in the lateral coital position.

When you are having intercourse in the lateral coital position, take advantage of the potential of the position. Since you are facing each other, use facial cues and communication to give information to your partner about your feelings and to enjoy the expressions of pleasure on your partner's face. You will have greater freedom of movement, because you don't have to support your partner's body weight. Use that freedom to move unhindered and use a variety of coital and touching movements. To increase your comfort and for physical support, you can use pillows under your head or to support your back. You should place these on the bed so they are in easy reach after you are in the lateral coital position.

One of the advantages of the position is that you have a very good and close access to your partner's body. In this position, more than in any other, you can touch and pleasure your partner non-genitally and genitally during intercourse. It is also easy to change who is initiating and controlling the rhythm of coital thrusting. During this exercise, try to work together so that the partner controlling the coital thrusting is at the same time being pleasured non-genitally and genitally. This can be a very sensual and sexually arousing experience. Of course, in subsequent experiences you can try other variations, e.g., the partner controlling thrusting also does the pleasuring. At least once during the intercourse, change the person who is directing the coital thrusting. One of the best ways to do this is that the partner switches rhythm or type of thrusting to be more in line with his needs. This is especially important for the woman who is able to engage more freely in the coital thrusting, and can do this in a way so as to be in harmony with and increase her level of sexual arousal. Also, this is an excellent position for the male to maintain ejaculatory control so that he can experience a good deal of sexual arousal without worrying about whether that will cause him to ejaculate too rapidly.

The couple should feel free to enjoy the sensations of the intercourse and not to press for rapid orgasm. Again, be aware that at each intercourse it is not mandatory that both partners achieve orgasm, but that orgasm is a natural result of sexual arousal. If orgasm is desired by both partners, this is an excellent position, since it is easier for the woman to have orgasm first because there is plenty of pelvic and indirect clitoral stimulation and the male can practice ejaculatory control. If the female desires further orgasms, it is also a good position to utilize the technique of manual clitoral stimulation to orgasm. One other thing might be mentioned: One of the most harmful myths in regard to intercourse and orgasm is that simultaneous orgasms are important. Setting simultaneous orgasms up as a goal is a major mistake. Since orgasm takes only three to ten seconds, striving to get that timing perfect takes away from the mutual experience of arousal, and it can be very frustrating if that goal is not achieved. Couples who accept simultaneous orgasm as being enjoyable when it occurs, but who are not bothered if it does not, will enjoy and accept their sexual intercourse and orgasm experiences in a much more reasonable and enhancing way.

This is also an excellent position for afterglow. Instead of switching positions, simply stay in the lateral coital position, continuing to touch each other and coming down together from your experience. Talk about your experience of working together and discuss the things that you might want to experiment with while using the lateral coital position. Then, if you wish, since it is a comfortable position, you can go off to sleep.

Again, we stress the idea that the lateral coital position might take some getting used to initially. For you and your partner to realize the sensual and sexual benefits, you will need to continue to refine and experiment with this position for a while. You should also be aware of, and feel comfortable with, exploring other varieties of side-by-side intercourse positions.

Fourth Set of Exercises For Chapter 13

Before beginning this exercise, it might be worth discussing some of the negative reactions you might have to this position. People mistakenly confuse the rear-entry intercourse position with anal intercourse. Rear entry simply means that the positioning is altered. The penis is inserted in the vagina, just as it is in other intercourse positions. Anal intercourse is quite different, in that the penis is inserted in the woman's anus. There is nothing abnormal or bizarre about anal intercourse. It is simply a variation in sexual technique that many couples find highly arousing and enjoyable.

If you and your partner have engaged in anal intercourse, take care to wash the penis with soap and water before placing it in her vagina. Many vaginal infections (Trichomonas vaginalis, Monilia, etc.) are caused by anal intercourse followed by vaginal intercourse without adequate washing.

Another misconception about the rear-entry position is that it represents a bestial orientation, since many animals do use rear-entry positioning for sexual activity. In reality, there is nothing bestial or primitive about rear-entry position. In fact, in the Scandinavian culture, which has one of the more liberated sexual climates, the rear-entry position is a favorite intercourse position.

A third common myth is that rear entry is a "homosexual" position, or that people who use it show latent homosexuality by doing so. This is a myth based on lack of sexual knowledge. What makes an act homosexual is the sex of the partners, not the technique used. Furthermore, homosexuals utilize anal intercourse, not rear-entry penile-vaginal intercourse.

With those misconceptions aside, discuss some of the advantages and discoveries you have available to you in the rear-entry position. One major advantage is that it allows the male considerable freedom in pleasing the female. The male's hands are quite free to caress, fondle, and stroke his partner's body both on her back and front. Another advantage is that many couples find the sensation of the male's body against the female's buttocks to be sensual, erotic, and pleasurable. The male can be free to massage the female's mons and clitoral area during intercourse. Also, a side-by-side variation of the rear-entry position is a minimally-exerting and comfortable sexual experience; for this reason, it is a good intercourse position during the later months of pregnancy.

There are many variations of this position, although this exercise will emphasize the lateral (side-by-side) rear-entry position. As you do this exercise, remember that your focus is on exploring and experiencing rather than testing your sexual powers or performance. To be comfortable with this position (as with others), you will need to be working together, sharing feelings, and discovering how this position can be enjoyable and a positive aspect of your relationship.

In the beginning of the exercise itself, you might want to start with a shower or bath, and be particularly aware of your reactions to the buttocks of your partner as you wash them. Let the foreplay and pleasuring interactions emphasize a free-flowing mutual sensual and sexual experience. Also, you might want to try some playful pleasuring — running your fingers through the woman's hair, drawing an imaginary circle on her body while kissing her, or tickling her feet. The female might try giving the male heavy, pleasurable fondling of his chest, stomach, shoulders, and genitals as she lies behind him with her body sensually resting against his back. The rubbing of her breasts against his upper back might provide new, enhancing sensations for both partners. When they are both feeling sexually aroused, the male positions himself behind his partner's body. As he is lying next to his partner, he can caress and fondle her breasts, neck, stomach, and mons area.

To position themselves for the lateral rear entry, each partner is lying on, say, the left side. They each bend their upper (right) legs, she extending her left leg to a comfortable position. The male extends his left leg behind him too, bending it slightly as he does so. When both partners are settled into a comfortable position, the male lifts his body high enough to guide intromission. As he guides his penis into the vaginal opening, the female can shift her body to help establish good penile containment. Especially during the first rear-entry experience, intromission should proceed slowly and unhurriedly. If you have any difficulty, do not panic or feel pressure. Remember, you are learning and exploring. After achieving intromission, the male can begin slow, rhythmic thrusting. He should be careful not to penetrate too deeply, since in the rear-entry position the vaginal canal is somewhat shorter than usual because of the female's body position. The female should feel free to guide her partner's manual caresses over her body. If she wishes to decrease the tempo or the depth of the male's body, thus affecting his thrusting movements. She can also influence the thrusting movements by moving her pelvis in harmony with her partner's thrusting. This will increase penile movement and feeling for both partners.

The male can enjoy caressing his partner's clitoral area as he continues the thrusting. This can be very arousing for her, and can often culminate in rapid orgasmic experiences. It is very important to be aware of whether the female desires an orgasmic experience during the intercourse, because when the male ejaculates in the rear-entry position, he often is unable to maintain penile containment afterward. However, if the male does ejaculate before his partner is orgasmic, he can easily use manual stimulation from that position so that his partner can have her first or additional orgasms. (Remember, though, that at every sexual encounter it is not crucial that both partners experience orgasm, and that being solely orgasm-directed can deprive both partners of a great many emotional, interpersonal, and sexual benefits.)

In this position, as any other sexual interaction, the afterglow period is very important to make it a whole sexual encounter. You might want to change positions for the afterglow experience so that you have better eye contact, and can visually experience your partner as you come down together. Discuss what things you really enjoyed — perhaps the male enjoyed the feeling of her buttocks against his genitals, or touching her back during intercourse; perhaps the female enjoyed the simultaneous manual and penile stimulation, or the pressure on her buttocks. You might want to discuss how you can experiment with variations of this position later.

Last Set of Exercises For Chapter 13

You might share some of your feelings and learnings from this series of exercises beginning with the self-exploration and the non-genital touch. You might want to highlight some of the positive feelings and reactions you have experienced. Spend a few minutes discussing what you have learned about yourself, your partner, and yourselves as a sensual and sexual couple.

We have tried to structure these exercises as guidelines, to provide an opportunity for you to learn, explore, and find what uniquely is comfortable and pleasurable for you. The process of exploring, being spontaneous, experimenting, and giving each other feedback should be a continuing one rather than ending with this series of exercises. This is just a foundation; you can continue to grow and enhance your relationship as a sensual and sexual couple. In this final exercise, we want you to do your own thing, putting together what you have learned about yourself and each other, but also being experimental and innovative with something that is uniquely yours. As a creative couple, you might focus your innovation in the area of pleasuring and foreplay, using a combination of oils in the pleasuring, having a whole day of heightened sensual activity, doing the pleasuring with all your clothes on, spending five minutes in totally sensual and sexually-arousing interactions, or anything that is uniquely you. Or you might focus on the intercourse interaction — trying out intercourse with the woman sitting and the male kneeling where he can massage his partner during intercourse, or with the couple in the sitting position (female lowers herself on her partner, who is seated on the bed or chair or thick carpet), or intercourse with both partners standing, or switching positions at least twice during intercourse, or any other intercourse variation or technique that you would like to experience. You might want to focus on the afterglow interaction. You could hold each other, with both your eyes closed, or sit nude and keep eye contact for five minutes, expressing with your eyes your feelings about the experience, or share an important secret about yourself that will help your partner understand you better, or try a different position to hold each other that is comfortable enough to sleep in, or anything else that will really cap your feelings of closeness and intimacy.

Once more we would like to emphasize that what we have presented in this book is a set of flexible guidelines and suggestions. Within the context of these shared experiences, you as a couple can decide what is beneficial and helpful for your relationship. It is you who can now better discuss even more rewarding and enhancing sensual and sexual experiences by being open to your feelings, sharing these with your partner, being willing to explore and experiment mutually, and then in being clear and direct in your responses to each other.

14 The Concept of Sexual Therapy

The material covered in this book is in some ways similar to the techniques you would be exposed to in receiving sexual therapy from a professional therapist. However, this book is *not* designed as a substitute for marital or sexual therapy. The exercises described in this book are designed for partners who function adequately, communicate fairly well, and can use the structure of the exercises to learn more about their sensual and sexual reactions. For those individuals and couples who have read this book or who have just glanced at it, and have decided that perhaps marital or sexual therapy might be more appropriate, we would like to describe how some forms of marital and sex therapy work. As you read, it is important to remember that approximately 50% of married couples experience sexual difficulties. Having a sexual problem is not something to be ashamed or embarrassed about, nor is it an insurmountable impediment. There are not enough competent, well-trained sex therapists to deal with all the couples who have problems. However, certified or licensed psychologists, marriage counselors, social workers, ministers, and psychiatrists can often be of great help in working with sexual problems.

For people considering sex counseling or therapy, the best way to obtain an appropriate referral is to call a local professional organization (local psychological association, a mental health association, or mental health clinic) or get a referral from a family physician, gynecologist or minister.

SEXUAL THERAPY MODELS

As a pivotal point for some of the following discussion, the sexual therapy approach of Masters and Johnson is important. The publication of their book *Human Sexual Response* in 1966 was a major breakthrough in the area of sexual information. Physicians and therapists at last had a base of information from which to evaluate the many sexual problems brought to them by clients. Even more exciting was the publication in 1970 of the clinical sequel to their research, *Human Sexual Inadequacy.* In this book they proposed, described, and evaluated a radically innovative model to treat sexual dysfunction clinically. In their model, the couple (all sex problems are considered couple problems) is seen daily for two weeks by a male-female therapy team, one of whom is a physician. Generally, the couple is requested not to be involved in work or child or family problems for these two weeks. (The rationale is that an intense two-week program to change sexual attitudes, feelings, and behavior is the most efficient way to do sex therapy.) Masters and Johnson are also involved in training sexual therapy teams.

Several people, including the senior author of this book, have proposed alternate models of engaging in sex therapy. Although the work of Masters and Johnson is an extremely exciting research and clinical breakthrough in sexual knowledge, there are some major problems in applying their procedure in a typical therapeutic practice. Chief among those is the issue of time and expense, especially for public mental health facilities. Also, the need for therapists to be physicians is questionable. There is no doubt that a physician should examine the individuals before the beginning of sex therapy to determine if there is any physiological cause for the sexual problem. However, in the great majority of cases the sexual problem results from insufficient learning, communication problems, or psychological difficulties. These are most appropriate for a non-medical therapist, such as a psychologist, social worker, marriage counselor, or minister.

The sexual therapy approach used by the senior author of this book utilizes a single therapist, seeing the couple once a week, and using the sex enhancement exercises described in this book — although with some appropriate modifications. We do feel that therapy outcome will be better if both partners are motivated and actively involved. The typical therapy sequence is that the couple is seen together first, usually for about half an hour to discuss the problem, to see if sex therapy is appropriate, and, if so, to define the goals of the therapy and establish the therapeutic contract. Then each partner (usually the one presenting the sexual problem) is seen alone to begin the sex history. However, as with Masters and Johnson, our view is that the complaint presented is actually the *couple's* problem, and not restricted to one of the partners. Typically sex histories take approximately one and one-half hours per person (the histories are done individually), and an attempt is made to put two sessions together or see the couple twice in a week so that the initial interview and the history are completed within a week. The couple is asked not to discuss the history-taking until the "round table feedback," although they are permitted to have sex as usual unless the sex has become so aversive that continuing sex activity would be antitherapeutic. Also, the clients are told to visit their own physicians to determine if there might be any physiological reason for sexual dysfunction.

During the next week there is another two-hour appointment for the round table feedback and to begin programming the sex-enhancement exercises. Thereafter, weekly appointments of one hour are scheduled. The clients are informed that if any difficulty does arise in doing exercises the couple should call the therapist. Since monitoring progress is more difficult in the once-a-week as opposed to daily-therapy basis, the telephone serves as a very convenient way to insure that if the clients misunderstand the instructions or have difficulty with a procedure, it does not have to be a wasted or negative week. In the senior author's experience, the typical sex therapy contract is between ten and fifteen sessions after the assessment phase. The history-taking, round-table concept, and sex therapy techniques utilized are all substantially based on the Masters and Johnson program.

A CASE HISTORY

Perhaps at this point a case illustration from the senior author's practice would be appropriate. The referring problem was Mrs. A's complaint of non-orgasmic response during five years of marriage. She had seen her minister, two gynecologists, and one psychiatrist for brief periods of time. (None had suggested sex therapy.) She was referred to the senior author by her neighbor, who was a student in the author's university psychology course, "Human Sexual Behavior." When the client called for an appointment, she was asked to bring her husband for the initial interview. Mr. and Mrs. A were a lower middle-class couple who were not very sophisticated psychologically. After a half-hour interview, they agreed there was a sexual problem which was causing them and their marriage a good deal of unhappiness, and that a direct sex therapy approach to the problem seemed most relevant. A history was begun with Mrs. A, and although she was anxious and embarrassed, she did attempt to respond directly during the interview. The following week, a

two-hour appointment was arranged; first the husband was
interviewed and then the wife. The clinical sex therapy model
seemed appropriate for this couple, since neither had major
psychological problems, and both had major sexual misconceptions
and were very uncommunicative about sex with each other. Mr. A
had no specific sexual dysfunction, but was markedly lacking in
knowledge of sexual techniques. During childhood and adolescence
he had received the message that sex was "fun but dirty, and not to
be talked about." Mrs. A harbored a great deal of guilt about
masturbation. In fact, she was situationally nonorgasmic rather than
primarily nonorgasmic, as she had maintained at first. Initially she
was too embarrassed to admit that she had masturbated to orgasm.
She had experienced rape, which had made a significant negative
impact on her view of sex. Generally, she was very unsure of her
sexuality. Sexual intercourse was attempted usually once every two
weeks, and Mrs. A found it very aversive. In this case the couple was
instructed not to have intercourse until the therapist deemed it
appropriate.

Before the round table feedback, each was seen
individually to get their permission to reveal secrets they had first
said they did not want the spouse to know. Both spouses had the
same secrets : both masturbated and both had considered having an
extra-marital affair. The therapist concentrated on the meaning of
the sexual problem and the need for a psycho-educational way of
learning to accept and respond to their sexuality and to give
responses to each other regarding what was pleasurable. The round
table feedback was the key to the treatment process. Rather than
placing sex in the context of guilt and making it a threat to
masculinity or femininity, it was redefined as an area of their lives in
which they had to learn as a couple to respond to each other. The
couple was then given the non-genital touching exercises, and told
that they should not view them as a rigid program, but rather as

adaptable guidelines. Mr. and Mrs. A moved through these procedures at a slower pace than most couples, but this seemed important for them, in that they needed a solid base of reawakened bodily feelings before they could move on. In fact, it took them into the third week before they were comfortable with the genital touching and pleasuring exercises. In addition to the couple exercises, Mrs. A was given the self-exploration and enhancement exercises. She had only masturbated by rubbing her knees together; she had never manually stimulated her vulval area. With Mrs. A, as with many other nonorgasmic females, the self-exploration and enhancement exercises were helpful in making her aware of her own responses and what turned her on sexually. She did the exercises privately at a different time than she did the exercises with her husband.

After this, appointments were made on a once-a-week basis. Each hour would begin with a recap of how the previous week's exercises had gone, including discussion of general, concerns and communication between the spouses, with the therapist encouraging them to be more open and specific in their feelings and sexual needs, and finally talking about the next set of exercises. (This weekly therapy session comprises the processes of monitoring progress, getting feedback, and helping the couple first to focus on any blocks to their sexual progress and then to work together to overcome them.)

Sexual therapy is built upon an ongoing professional contact between the therapist and his clients. The supportive and instructional functions of the therapist cannot be achieved by a book. That is why we remind you that you should not rely only upon our exercises if you have persistent and troubling sexual difficulties.

After the third weekly therapy session, Mrs. A was regularly orgasmic during manual masturbation and feeling better about herself and her ability to respond. Also, Mr. and Mrs. A had a better understanding of both their own and their spouses' sexual responses. The fourth session focused on the exercises for increasing arousal and sexual responsivity for women. Two days after that session, the therapist received a call from Mrs. A saying that she didn't understand one of the non-demand positions. The position was reexplained over the phone; they were told to try it again and if it still felt uncomfortable to discontinue it for the week and to focus on other genital pleasuring exercises. However, after the telephone consultation the problem was resolved. (This illustrates another advantage of having consulted a professional therapist.)

The fifth session introduced the oral-genital exercises. There was some reluctance on Mrs. A's part to attempt this. During the session her reluctance was related to a past negative experience with oral sex which had been discussed in the sex history. Having this information available to both partners made it easier to alter the program and reemphasize the importance of Mr. A's support. Mrs. A was told that oral-genital sex was something which could be tried, that many couples did enjoy it, and that she couldn't know her reactions until it was attempted with Mr. A's support. She was told that if she became anxious, she could move back to manual-genital touch. Mr. A made it clear that he would not reject her if she decided that she did not like oral-genital sex. During the next two sessions reactions to various stimulatory techniques were discussed, feelings and attitudes explored, and by the end of the eighth week she was orgasmic with both manual and oral stimulation.

The ninth therapy session was spent discussing changes in the couple's marital relationship and communication patterns. Even in sex therapy, where the major focus is on relearning sexual comfort and response, the marital and personal factors do come into focus and are discussed. Often a major factor in the success of sex therapy is the couple's improved communication process. The major difference between marital and sex therapy is that the former involves greater emphasis on the communication process in the relationship, and focuses as well on important non-sexual issues.

By the tenth week, a specific program for intercourse was initiated using the increasing arousal and comfort in intercourse exercises. The couple had been having intercourse since the sixth week, but were doing it separately from the pleasuring and exercise program. The question of when and how to have intercourse while engaged in the sexuality program is one for the individuals concerned, and it is discussed by the couple and therapist in the first or second session. Intercourse was initiated using the female superior position to encourage Mrs. A to be more sexually expressive. During the next two weeks the couple worked on integrating their pleasuring and foreplay techniques into different intercourse positions, including the lateral coital position. By the twelfth week, Mrs. A was functioning orgasmically during both foreplay and intercourse. The final two sessions were used to integrate what they had learned about themselves individually, their functioning as a couple, and how to continue to enhance their sexuality. Termination occurred after the fourteenth session, approximately three months after therapy began. On a three month follow-up, they reported that not only had the orgasmic responses and their enjoyment of sex continued, but that their entire relationship, including their relationship with their children, had continued to improve.

Of course, not all couples work as smoothly as this couple did. They were well-motivated and basically had a good marital relationship. This couple was seen for three months; some couples are seen for as few as one or two interviews, while others are seen for more than a year.

To help the reader understand the breadth and complexity of the sex therapy approach as well as when marriage counseling or individual psychotherapy might be more appropriate, several other cases will be briefly described. *It should be recognized that sex therapy is a specific technique, and that sometimes even though there is a sexual difficulty, another method of helping might be more appropriate.*

THERAPY FOR AN OLDER COUPLE

Mr. and Mrs. R were an older married couple: He was 63 and she was 57. They had been married thirty-six years; it was the second marriage for him and the first for her. During both of his marriages he experienced recurrent problems with premature ejaculation and difficulty in maintaining erections. Although she was occasionally orgasmic, she found sexual activity, and specifically intercourse, to be quite unsatisfying. Despite the sexual difficulties they reported a generally satisfying marriage and had successfully raised three children. (It might be noted that it is not at all unusual for individuals to function quite well interpersonally and maritally, and yet to have very unsatisfying sex lives.)

When they read about sex therapy in various magazines, Mr. and Mrs. R decided to check with their physician to get his recommendation. Like all too many physicians (and ministers, social workers, psychiatrists, and psychologists), he disregarded their request for sexual information and counseling, with the comment that at their age sex should not be that important. This delayed their seeking help for two years, but eventually they did contact the senior author. He was very impressed with both their motivation for change and their obvious caring for each other and ability to work together. Although they communicated well in most areas of their lives, at the levels of sexual communication and feelings they were very inept. It was not that they did not *want* to communicate sexually; it was much more that they did not know how to. In our initial meetings, we discussed some of the myths they held about sexuality, the specific effects of aging on sexual functioning, and desensitization to the use of sexual words. During the first two weeks they worked on the non-genital and genital pleasuring exercises. In many ways, they were the easiest couple that the senior author has ever worked with. They supported each other extremely well and they were open and non-defensive; and although their initial skill level was low, they were excellent learners. By the end of the genital touching and pleasuring exercises, the couple was feeling good about each other, feeling good about their sexuality, and feeling good about the therapy.

They then focused on the exercises regarding sex and the aging couple. In fact, their evaluations contributed much to the chapter which appears in this book. Altogether, we met nine times and completed the exercises mentioned plus the exercises on ejaculatory control and intercourse. When they left therapy, that did not mean they stopped enhancing their sexual functioning. On their own, they agreed to pursue exercises on improving arousal and orgasmic functioning for the woman as well as increasing comfort with oral-genital stimulation and non-demand pleasuring. There is no doubt in their minds nor the therapist's that they will continue to enjoy their sexuality for years to come.

THERAPY INAPPROPRIATE IN ONE CASE

After reviewing these two successful cases, let us look at a case where sex therapy was not appropriate. Mr. and Mrs. C were referred specifically for sex therapy. They had been married four years, and reported that their sexual adjustment was quite good premaritally (they had been having intercourse for two years before marriage), and had continued good for the first three years of the marriage. However, during the last year it had become markedly poorer both in terms of quantity and quality. Neither reported a specific sexual dysfunction, but both reported experiencing less pleasure during sexual interaction and Mrs. C specifically reported a decreased desire for intercourse.

During the initial interview and history taking, it

became apparent that the sexual problem was enmeshed in a very complex web of personal and marital difficulties. Mrs. C enjoyed her role as a mother (they had a small child), but found herself missing her job and the social interactions it had offered. Mr. C was quite dissatisfied with his present job, as well as being concerned with problems revolving around the health of his parents. Also, they were unhappy with their social life as a couple and worried about financial matters since they now had a home but only one salary. Rather than talking about these issues, Mr. and Mrs. C ignored them; the problems worsened, and this directly affected their sexual functioning.

The therapist decided to work on the sexual problem directly, and hoped that in the process they could begin communicating again and this would carry over to their marital communication and discussing other problem areas. At first, this strategy seemed to be working; they enjoyed the pleasuring activities and reported more sexual arousal than in months. However, as we went on, the sexual relationship seemed to reach a plateau, higher than before they came for sex therapy, but still quite a bit less enjoyable than when they were first married. We discussed this with the couple, and we agreed to change the focus of our sessions from sex to marital therapy. In subsequent sessions, we talked more about their personal concerns regarding money, relations with in-laws, and their future career plans. Also, attempts were made to clarify their expectations of each other and to adopt more flexible roles in their relationship, especially in regard to Mr. C's increasing his responsibility for taking care of their child. As they worked out these problems and began communicating more, the sexual functioning also improved. Although we did not spend much time in the session on the exercises, the couple did use the sexual enhancement exercises on their own. We terminated our sessions after about eight months (which is longer than the typical sex therapy approach), with a couple feeling better about themselves as people, as a married couple, and as a sexually functioning couple.

A CASE WHERE THERAPY FAILED

Let us now look at a case with unsuccessful results. Mr. and Mrs D were referred by Mr. D's psychiatrist, who had been treating him for depression and excessive drinking. Mr. D had had a ten-year history of secondary impotence problems* and in the past two years had been able to complete intercourse with his wife only about five times. He was interested in working to improve his arousal and potency, but Mrs. D was quite ambivalent. She was both angry at him and disappointed with him. Specifically, they fought over money, his lack of attention to the children, his past extra-marital affairs, and the fact that they spent little time together. She firmly believed that things would get better "if he would pay more attention to me and try harder." Attempts to define the problem as a couple-problem with the orientation that they needed to work together and support each other were not successful. Although we talked about the non-genital touching exercises, and they agreed to try them, they did not, and did not return for further sessions. This exhibits the crucial factor of the need for motivation to change. Sometimes, sexual problems are enmeshed in personal and marital problems of long standing. They can be remedied by marital or sex therapy, or they may require individual psychotherapy. However, the person and couple must be motivated to work together and support each other in attempting these changes.

---

*A man with secondary impotence has had at least one successful intercourse experience, involving potency, but is now losing or failing to get erections twenty-five to thirty percent of the time.

SEXUAL THERAPY FOR OTHER THAN MARRIED COUPLES

The theories and practices illustrated in this book can be applied to situations involving persons other than married couples, because every person, whether he is part of a marriage team or not, possesses sexuality. We draw upon our therapy experience to give a few examples of persons whose sexual functioning has been improved with professional assistance.

GAY COUPLES

The authors have never treated a gay couple using these sex enhancement exercises; however, we are aware of several gay couples who have used them on their own and found them relevant and rewarding. Especially useful are the exercises on non-genital touching, genital touching and pleasuring, increasing arousal for women, increasing arousal and potency for males, the non-demand exercises, and the oral-genital stimulation exercises. The senior author has worked with a single individual, however, and will briefly describe that case. The client, Mr. E, was 32, had been involved in a gay lifestyle for over ten years, and was presently living with his lover of two years. During the past several months he had been experiencing increasingly severe anxiety attacks as well as intermittent impotence. He consulted the senior author about the anxiety states, but it was quickly determined that the anxiety and the sexual relationship were intricately related. When he was unable to perform sexually, he felt very anxious, afraid his lover would leave him, and afraid he had somehow lost his masculinity. This anxiety began to interfere with his work relationships, and he feared that the quality of his work had declined to the extent that he might be fired. It was decided to see Mr. E alone, rather than with his partner, because the partner was not very interested in coming to the sessions and there were practical scheduling problems. However, Mr. E's partner did agree to participate in the sex enhancement exercises. It was evident that Mr. E's anxiety and tension and concerns about sexual performance were inhibiting his sexual arousal. He felt very pressured by his partner to perform, and throughout the sexual interchange he was being a bystander in the sense of observing his response and worrying about his erection. Treatment consisted of making him aware that he was in a self-defeating cycle, teaching him deep muscle relaxation techniques, and of having him go through the sex enhancement exercises with his partner. Mr. E discovered to both his surprise and pleasure that when he was instructed that he didn't have to carry through the sexual interchange to orgasm (so the pressure was off), he was not anxious and he developed and maintained good erections. He needed to be reminded and coaxed to practice the exercise of allowing his erection to decrease and then regain it, but after doing the sequence two or three times his self-confidence in his sexual responses soared. Therapy was terminated after three and one-half months. Mr. E had improved feelings about his sexual functioning; these feelings reduced his anxiety and improved his functioning in his work situation.

UNMARRIED COUPLES

Although the majority of clinical sex therapy is done with married couples, we have also had experience with unmarried couples. Based on our experience, we feel that unmarried couples who have some commitment to each other and who can communicate about the relationship can benefit quite well from sex therapy. However, couples who have a tenuous relationship and whose communication pattern is deficient often use sex therapy and exercises as a battleground for other problems, and this very much interferes with developing better feelings and attitudes about their own sexuality.

One unmarried couple seen in therapy had been going together for three years, and living together on weekends for the past year. They reported a relatively strong commitment to each other, but felt no urgency to marry and were hesitant about making such a binding commitment. The sexual difficulty was situational non-orgasmic response in the woman, Ms. F. She had been orgasmic during masturbation, was occasionally orgasmic during foreplay, but had never been orgasmic during intercourse. This is a fairly common sexual problem for women, and one of the more difficult to treat. The first thing emphasized to both Mr. G and Ms. F was that it was perfectly normal and healthy to have orgasms by techniques other than intercourse, and that since all orgasms, whether through foreplay, oral stimulation, intercourse, or afterplay are the same they should not put pressure on her to be orgasmic during intercourse. Mr. G, like many other males, seemed to feel he was a "poor lover" if his partner were not orgasmic during intercourse. It was emphasized that this was a cruel myth that was causing both of them unneeded and non-productive psychological distress. Treatment focused on having both of them develop a more broad-ranging understanding of their own and their partner's sensual and sexual responses. Also emphasized was the more effective and comfortable use of oral-genital sexual stimulation. He was quite ineffective in cunnilingus, and she felt too inhibited to give him negative response and to guide him to perform cunnilingus in a slower, more arousing manner. In fact, four sessions were devoted to improving feedback skills in oral-genital stimulation. After four and a half months of treatment, Ms. F was regularly orgasmic in the foreplay and pleasuring interactions, often experiencing multi-orgasmic responses, occasionally being orgasmic during intercourse, and occasionally during afterglow. The couple had lowered their unrealistically high expectations of each other's sexual performance, were much less uptight with the sexual interactions which did not go particularly well, and found themselves beginning to develop their own unique style of sexual interaction. The sex therapy seemed to strengthen their relationship and commitment. Other couples with whom the authors have worked found that the sex therapy experience made them aware of incompatibility and unmet expectations; this awareness resulted in dissolution of the couple's relationship.

SINGLE INDIVIDUALS

Though a great deal of sex therapy is done with couples, there are specialized and effective techniques used with individuals who are not involved in an ongoing relationship, but who would like some professional help in dealing with sexual difficulties. Such individuals might view their sexual problems as being an obstacle to their being involved in a relationship, or they might actively avoid relationships because they have experienced difficulties in the past. At times, sex therapists utilize techniques with their clients to help deal with interpersonal anxiety, communication difficulties, and subjectively felt social and sexual conflicts. For example, along with a specific sex therapy program, the therapist and client might discover that the client might profit from assertive training in order for him to establish or improve social contacts. In such situations the client and therapist might engage in a technique called *behavioral rehearsal*, with the goal being to develop more appropriate social skills which carry over into the "real world." Not uncommonly, the therapist might help a client to expand his or her sexual awareness by outlining self-enhancement exercises such as those set forth in this book. The self-enhancement programs can be enormously beneficial in helping the individual to accept and enjoy sexuality as a vital part of life. As mentioned in the introductory chapter of this book, if a person is not involved in a meaningful relationship, there can still be profit from reading this book in terms of attitude change. If you as an individual feel that the self-enhancement exercises are suitable for you, then you might go through them. Beyond that, if you feel that conflicts or anxieties are somehow hampering fuller awareness of your sexuality, you are likely to profit from consulting with a professional therapist.

The senior author has treated several single individuals in sex therapy without partners. Several women who have never been orgasmic and doubted their womanhood and capacity to function sexually have learned to be orgasmic through the use of the self-enhancement exercises, often along with the use of a vibrator to provide the initial intense stimulation.

Sex therapy can help in integrating feelings of sexuality into one's personal lifestyle as well as discussing how to develop better interpersonal and sexual relationships with partners.

Probably the most common single-person sex therapy client is the male with potency problems. Mr. H was a rather typical client. He had a history of lack of sex education, felt uncomfortable around women, but had experienced successful intercourse with several women. Although the intercourse was successful, generally the relationships, the communication during sex, and the inclusion of sensual foreplay and afterplay were minimal or entirely absent from the sexual interactions. During one sexual interaction in his early twenties, he was uninterested in the woman, found her sexually unattractive, but since she was willing to have intercourse, he pursued it and found that he lost his erection and was not able to proceed with intercourse. Instead of realizing that occasional potency problems are normal and that on this occasion it was very understandable that he was not sexually aroused, he became very anxious and concerned that he would never be able to perform well sexually again. The next night he went out with a woman with whom he had had successful intercourse earlier. She was a very demanding woman, and this combined with his performance anxiety resulted in a second unsuccessful experience. From then on, at each meeting with a woman his central concern was whether he would be able to perform if they got to the bed. During the next three years, his social and sexual life deteriorated. Although he occasionally completed intercourse, generally he lost or never got erections and at each "failure" experience he berated himself and his "failed manhood." With his lowered self-esteem and self-confidence he was even more anxious around women. He was enmeshed in a very self-defeating cycle.

Before being seen for treatment, he was referred to a urologist who found no physiological or medical impediments to sexual functioning, and Mr. H found this reassuring. He was also encouraged by the therapist's information that impotence did not have to be a chronic problem. Since the therapist did not utilize female surrogate partners, treatment consisted of desensitizing Mr. H's anxieties, using imagery techniques, having him read and discuss several of the sex enhancement exercises, and discussing the development of relationships with women that focus on sensual and affectionate interchange between partners is a non-demanding, non-performance-oriented atmosphere. As treatment progressed, Mr. H stopped putting himself down sexually and reported less anxiety and more confidence around women. His sexual functioning improved somewhat, but he continued to have intermittent potency problems. On the other hand, he was no longer afraid to establish relationships with women, and his hope, as well as the therapist's, was that in a good, stable relationship he could function without potency problems and could develop his sensual and sexual responses and enjoy his sexuality.

SEXUALITY AND YOU, THE READER

What should be emphasized is that you as an individual and as a couple have a right to understand and be comfortable with your own sexuality. Your sexual behavior should be a positive part of your life and serve to enrich your personality rather than be a cause of problems. The purpose of this book is to help people learn about and understand their sexuality; if this approach does not fulfill your needs, by all means feel comfortable in seeking professional help. Rather than a sign of weakness, seeing a professional therapist is a sign of strength and a healthy desire to solve your personal and sexual difficulties.

Last, remember that you are a sexual person from the day you are born to the day you die. Your sexuality is an important and integral part of you as a person. Allow it to be a positive part of your life.

Suggested Readings for Further Information

1.   Belliveau, F., & Richter, L. *Understanding Human Sexual Inadequacy.* New York: Bantam, 1970. A book describing the basic research and clinical work of Masters and Johnson. Easy to read and aimed toward the lay public.

2.   Boston Women's Health Collective. *Our Bodies, Our Selves.* New York: Simon and Schuster, 1973. An excellent book on sexuality written by, for, and about women.

3.   Brecher, E. M. *The Sex Researchers.* New York: Signet, 1971. A history of sex education and research, focused on a personal look at the pioneers in the field.

4.   Comfort, A. *The Joy of Sex.* New York: Crown, 1972. A sophisticated, somewhat esoteric book about advanced sexual techniques. Excellent for liberated, experimenting couples.

5.   Downing, G. *The Massage Book.* New York: Random House, 1972. One of the best books on the art of sensual massage.

6.   Gordon, S. *The Sexual Adolescent*. Belmont: Duxburg, 1973. An excellent book for teachers, counselors, or parents in understanding adolescent sexuality. Particularly good chapter on masturbation.

7.   Guttmacher, A. *Pregnancy, Birth, and Family Planning*. New York: Viking Press, 1973. An excellent source book for information on contraception and family planning.

8.   Hartmann, W. E., & Fithian, M. A. *Treatment of Sexual Dysfunction*. Long Beach: Center for Marital and Sexual Studies, 1972. A description of a two-week sex therapy program written for sex therapists. Use of wide variety of techniques, including audio-visual.

9.   Kaplan, H.S. *The New Sex Therapy*. New York: Brunner/Mazel, 1974. An attempt to integrate traditional psychotherapeutic viewpoints with sex therapy techniques. Interesting case studies; however, weak in description and understanding of behavioral procedures.

10.   Katchadourian, H. A., & Lunde, D. T. *Fundamentals of Human Sexuality*. New York: Holt, Rinehart, and Winston, 1972 A comprehensive text on human sexuality, useful for college students or the lay public.

11.   Masters, W. H., & Johnson, V. A. *Human Sexual Response*. Boston: Little, Brown, 1966. Landmark text on the basic physiology of human sexual response. Difficult for lay public to read.

12.   Masters, W. H., & Johnson, V. A. *Human Sexual Inadequacy*. Boston: Little, Brown, 1970. An excellent text for professionals describing a pioneer sex therapy program.

13. McCary, J. L. *Sexual Myths and Fallacies*. New York: Van Nostrand, 1971. A very readable book describing all of the most common and some very unusual sex myths.

14. McCary, J. L. *Human Sexuality* (Second Edition). New York: Van Nostrand, 1973. Perhaps the best of the comprehensive books on human sexual behavior. Written for college students as well as the lay public.

15. *Population and the American Future: Report of the Commission on Population and the American Future.* New York: New American Library, 1972. A comprehensive report on sex, sex education, contraception, and the population program. An excellent book.

16. Rubin, I., & Calderwood, D. *A Family Guide to Sex*. New York: Signet, 1973. A sensitively written book, especially good in terms of sex education issues.

17. Schiller, P. *Creative Approach to Sex Education and Counseling*. New York: Association Press, 1973. A very good book for professionals in the area of sex education and counseling.